ADVENTURES BEYOND YOUR WILDEST IMAGINATION ARE YOURS FOR THE ASKING . . .

This is the third volume in the bestselling *How to Win at Nintendo Games* series. To those of you just getting your feet wet in the unforgettable world of Nintendo games, we bid you welcome. To those battle-scarred veterans who have died a thousand fiery deaths: we're glad you're back. Before you get back in front of that video screen, let's sit down for a few minutes, catch our breaths and chat.

Jeff Rovin, the author of *How to Win at Nintendo Games I* and *II,* is back again with more handpicked favorites from the vast Nintendo games archives—as well as Tengen's game *Super Sprint.* The hottest games are all here, including *Castlevania II: Simon's Quest, Guardian Legend, Bad Dudes,* and *Ninja Gaiden.* The book starts off with *The Adventures of Bayou Billy* and finishes in a flash with an all-new special update section—featuring the scoop on *Super Mario Bros. 2: Complete Guide to Worlds 4–7,* not to mention *Teenage Mutant Ninja Turtles!*

What more could an honest, hard-fighting videogame adept ask for? It's all here but the experiencing—and the winning! That's up to you!

HOW TO WIN AT NINTENDO®GAMES III

St. Martin's Paperbacks titles
by Jeff Rovin

HOW TO WIN AT NINTENDO GAMES
HOW TO WIN AT NINTENDO GAMES II
HOW TO WIN AT NINTENDO GAMES III

HOW TO WIN AT NINTENDO GAMES #3

Jeff Rovin

ALSO INCLUDES THE TENGEN GAME, *SUPER SPRINT*

ST. MARTIN'S PAPERBACKS

How to Win at Nintendo® Games III is an unofficial guide, not endorsed by Nintendo®.

Nintendo is a registered trademark of Nintendo of America Inc.

HOW TO WIN AT NINTENDO GAMES III

Copyright © 1990 by Jeff Rovin.

ISBN: 0-312-92215-9

Printed in the United States of America

St. Martin's Paperbacks edition/April 1990

10 9 8 7 6 5 4 3 2 1

ACKNOWLEDGMENTS

Deepest gratitude to the following, who shared their vast knowledge of Nintendo games: Aaron Berkowitz (the Broomall Basher), Shepard Boucher, Steve Menniti, Ryan Quirk, Marcel Herrera, the DiFates (Victor, Chris, and Roseanne—but not Vincent, who doesn't know a joystick from a pretzel stick) (hint: the joystick is the one without the salt), Michael Gordon (the Ace of Rt. 1), Mark Skyer, Jordan Davis, Robert Skidmore, Travis Nelson, Eva Rupert, and Bill Abram of Abram & Yagoda Systems Group, Tarrytown, NY—who knows more about software than any other mortal. Special thanks to Samuel and Michael, who made the supreme sacrifice of not practicing the piano and violin, and even staying up past their bedtimes, so they could struggle through some of these games.

CONTENTS

INTRODUCTION

Three has always been a magic number to Nintendo game fans.

Most games start you off with three lives.

You have to work three controllers to play (joystick, A and B button).

There are three games in the Super Mario Brothers series (though the third cartridge isn't available in the U.S. yet, just in Japan).

And now, to get the 1990s off to a rip-roaring start, there are three volumes of *How to Win at Nintendo Games!*

We've made just one change from the earlier books. After reading your letters, we've decided to expand our NINTEN-DO'S AND DON'T'S section at the end of the book. It now contains more tips on more games than ever before!

As in our other two books, here's what you'll find when you look up individual games in the main section of the book:

Type: the kind of game it is (fantasy quest, commando raid, space combat, etc.).

1

Manufacturer: who made the game.

Objective: what the game's about.

Layout: what you'll see on the screen.

Hero: the character's powers and weaknesses.

Enemies: who's who among your foes, and what kind of abilities they have.

Menu: game variations.

Scoring: what kind of points, extra lives, extra weapons, extra time, etc., you can receive or lose.

Beginner's Strategy: tips for someone who's just starting out.

Advanced Strategy: a guide for the more experienced player.

Par: how far the average player should expect to get.

Training Tips: specific exercises and tips for how to improve your performance in the game.

Rating: if you're thinking of buying or renting the cartridge, this section will tell you whether or not it's worth it. Grades are A,B,C,D, and F.
Challenge: is the game easy to master?
Graphics: are they eye-popping, or could you do better with an Etch-a-Sketch?
Sound Effects: does the music sound orchestral, or like a kazoo? Does that car engine sound like a mighty V8, or like a toy from a cereal box?

Whether you're reading this book with your Nintendo Entertainment System turned on or while driving in the car on a long trip to Grandma's—turn the page to scale new heights of videogaming excitement!

CHAPTER ONE

THE ADVENTURES OF BAYOU BILLY

Type: Swampland shoot-'em-up and race game.

Manufacturer: Konami, under license from Nintendo.

Objective: Because lawman Billy has been hurting the operation of smuggler Gordon, the gangster kidnaps Billy's girlfriend Annabelle. As Billy, your latest bit of crimebusting is to make your way through the countryside to Gordon's plantation, where Annabelle is being held.

Layout: There are nine different levels. The screen scrolls horizontally in one, three, six, eight, and nine; you look out from Billy's eyes in the gun-shooting levels (two and seven) and driving screens (four and five).

Hero: Billy can acquire four different weapons, though he can only pack the Gun and one other at any given time. He also collects Survival Gear, like Bullets and First-Aid Boxes.

5

These are detailed in the instructions and also below.

Enemies: You'll be facing "Gordon's Groupies" (a dumb name, given the context), a bunch of muscular men, each of whom has various strengths and weapons. These, as well as the slew of attack vehicles you'll face, are described in the instructions and also below.

Menu: In the shooting sections you can choose to fire using either the controller or the Light Gun. There is only a one-player game.

Scoring: You receive points for killing enemies, and you also win extra lives when you collect 20,000 points, and at every 10,000-point plateau thereafter.

Beginner's Strategy: Be aware of one thing before starting: when you throw the Knife, your enemy can pick it up and use it against you. Be prepared to jumpkick it from their hand before it's thrown.

To get through the first level, do the following. Go to the far right and immediately hit Tolouse with six fast jumpkicks. He'll go down. When you come up against the next two thugs, get between them and jumpkick from side to side. For the next trio, stop where the grass and dirt meet and use the jumpkick left and right to defeat them. One of these flunkies will give you Food when he's beaten, which boosts your energy. Kick or punch the Birds, which fly by next, then go into the water and fight the Crocs, using punches. One of them will give you more Food. Jumpkick the next trio of killers into dreamland, and pick up the Ugly Stick to finish the job, if necessary. The next guy approaches from the left, with a Knife. Be alert for his arrival, and either dodge the Knife or disarm the man if you're close enough. Take the blade if you want to be able to kill long distance (as opposed to having to get in and rumble with the Ugly Stick). At the pond, toss the Knife to the other side (between the two ponds) as you fight the Crocs (your punch is more effective; so's the Stick, if you decided to keep that instead of the Knife). When you're between the two ponds, pick up the Knife. You'll be assaulted here by a slew of diving-suited Jacques, who will come at you from both sides. It's okay to get in the water and mix it up: you'll be at no disadvantage here, and it'll take slightly longer for the divers from the other pond to get to you. You'll get a Gun from one of the dead Jacques. Toward the end of the battle, Hurricane Hank will come wading along. Shoot him twice, and he's fish food. More Jacques will arrive shortly; upon dying, one of them will give you the Bulletproof Vest. When you reach the third pond, you may be low on energy. If you are, and don't want to risk fighting the Crocs, simply cross using repeated jumpkicks. Your energy will be restored at the end of the level.

Level two is relatively simple whether you're using the controller or the light gun. All you have to do is aim and fire! If you have the Bulletproof Vest, you're sure to get through okay. You can also obtain a 1-Up, a First-Aid Kit, the Hourglass (keeps you from running out of Bullets), and extra Bullets. At the clearing, the Whirlybird arrives; shoot at it, but stop at once when people appear, and deal with them first. Then turn your fire back on the chopper. It will take approximately sixty shots to bring the Whirlybird down.

Level three is more or less a rerun of the first level. Use the jumpkick and Knife on your first two adversaries, kill the Crocs in the first pond (you can't skip these: their death enables you to pass to the next screen), punch out the Birds you encounter, then use jumpkicks to fell the two Thugs McGraws. Get Food from the next two baddies, then be on the lookout for the next trio. Two of the men will come from the right, tossing Knives. Your Bulletproof Vest will protect you, but if you don't have it, be prepared to move up or down to dodge the blades! Get one of the Knives and use it on them. Next up: Luis Tor-Ture, who's quite a bruiser. He'll try to grab you and toss you in the air; landing on your head will cost you energy! What you have to do is go to the right at once and attack him while he's still there. Use a flurry of punches, hitting him over and over, and he'll go down without landing a single blow! Alas, though your dear Annabelle is within sight, she gets pushed into a truck and driven off. Thus, it's time to hop in your car and go after her.

Advanced Strategy: Levels four and five are played against a timer: you have 99 seconds to reach the end of the road, or you lose a life. Also on both levels you'll encounter Rocks, other Cars, skid-causing Oil Puddles, and Bomb-laden aircraft (Smuggling Planes on four, Whirlybirds on five), which come more or less at random.

On level four, more often than not, Rocks will appear in the road when there's approximately 77 seconds, 57 seconds, 50 seconds, and 36 seconds left on the clock—assuming you're keeping up a pace of 180 miles per hour on the straightaways and approximately 140 miles per hour on the turns. If you're not going that fast, you'll have trouble reaching the end of the course in time. Occasionally, the Rocks will appear as late as 45 seconds remaining, but that's rare. Puddles usually don't appear in level four until near the end, usually with 29 and 17 seconds remaining. On level five don't bother trying to note the time at which these objects come; there's too many of them, the vehicles move faster, you'll be watching for the Gasoline Cans you'll need to complete the course, and the road twists and turns a great deal more. So forget about the timer. (Ignoring the timer is also something you'll probably do in the closing seconds of level four, when, in addition to dealing with sudden sharp turns, you'll face the Smuggling Planes which now come at you in pairs.)

The big problem on both of these tracks is the vehicular traffic. You'll be shooting the cars into scrap metal, so you don't have to drive around them. Problem is, from a distance the Rocks look just like Cars—and you can't shoot those! So be prepared to cut a hard left or right to get around the Rocks (usually a right, since almost all of the Rocks appear on the left of the road, with a few in the center). It isn't a bad idea to routinely swerve around every road obstacle you shoot at. If it's a Car and explodes, no harm was done maneuvering around it.

Another choice you'll have is whether to ignore the aircraft and dodge their Bombs, or shoot at the aircraft and thus remove the threat of explosives. If you choose the latter, you'll have to swerve around any Cars you may encounter, since you can't lob Grenades into the air and fire your Guns simultaneously. After repeated runs down the fifth-level course, we've decided that the best approach is to shoot at the Whirlybirds rather than to swerve around the Bombs. It's better to risk the possibility that a Rock or Car may appear in that time than to face the certainty that Bombs will be dropped!

Overall, a key aspect to surviving on levels four and five is to make small adjustments so you'll stay to the center of the road as you round all curves. Otherwise, chances are good that you'll sideswipe or plow into the posts that line the side of the road.

Level six is a return to the side view of the first level, though it features more and tougher foes. There's more or less a standard way of dealing with the goons you'll face early. Disarm them with a jumpkick, then use your Whip to lash them senseless. It'll work quicker than any other weapons you possess. Several Migrane Mikes appear on this level, swinging a ball and chain; they glow red before they start whirling the mace, so you've got about two seconds to hit them before they attack. If you can't disable a Mike before he starts to swing the weapon, come up from beneath him and get in close, using a normal kick to the midsection to beat him. Toward the end of the level you'll also have to get your enemies out of their Bulletproof Vests in order to defeat them. Use jumpkicks for this. When more than one foe is around, don't focus on just one enemy or the others will get you. Make sure you yourself have a Vest as you reach the area of the third Bar, since just about everyone you meet will be packing a weapon.

Level seven is more of the same, though this time you have foes coming at you from inside buildings (through the windows) and from beneath manhole covers. Keep an eye on these as you pass. Also make sure you get the man on the motorcycle. What he's carrying will be of interest to you. Levels eight and nine are simply tougher versions of what's come before; if you've gotten this far, you understand all the techniques and strategies and should have no trouble.

Par: A good player will be able to complete most of the fourth level. An average score of 13,000 points per level is good.

Training Tips: Go to the Training Mode and practice your jumpkick. That's the skill you'll need the most in this game. Also, when you get your hands on each new weapon, give it a try and see how it works. On the driving stages, go through them in slow motion (with the NES Advantage), so you can get a look at the road.

Rating: There are shooting games and driving games, but few cartridges offer both skills . . . both of which are well done. The fact that you can also use the light gun in this game is a definite plus.

Challenge: B+

Graphics: C+ (the animation is phooey on the shooting stages, and there's too much image breakup. The driving phases are good, however.)

Sound Effects: B—

CHAPTER TWO

ADVENTURES OF LOLO

Type: Fantasy quest.

Manufacturer: HAL America, Inc., under license from Nintendo.

Objective: Princess Lala has been abducted by the Great Devil—who also intends to destroy the country of Eden. Prince Lolo sallies forth to the Devil's Haunted Castle, to negotiate its mazes, fight its monstrous denizens, and teach the Great Devil a lesson. You hope.

Layout: Each screen is a separate room, seen from overhead; there are ten floors in the Castle, with five rooms on each. Lolo can move in any direction in each room.

Hero: Lolo "is not blessed with strength or agility," just "great courage, high IQ, and a lot of patience." Fortunately, inside the Castle, he'll encounter Heart Framers (Hearts inside little frames), most of which give him the ability to shoot monsters and turn them into Eggs (a second shot boots the Eggs off the screen entirely); Special Heart Framers, which give him Magic Shots; Emerald Framers, which allow him to block or imprison monsters; Eggs, which is what the shot-monsters become for 6 seconds, and which allow Lolo to cross Rivers; Bridges, for getting across Rivers or Lava; Hammers, for destroying Rocks; and Flower Beds, which don't move, but which Lolo can use to hide from monsters. Once Lolo has cleared the room of all Hearts, a Treasure Chest will open. When the hero reaches it, all the monsters will be destroyed.

Enemies: The eight different monsters scattered throughout the Castle are discussed in the instructions, and also below. Also working against you are One-Way Arrows. You can only pass over these in the direction they're pointing—unless you've acquired a One-Way Pass from a Special Heart Framer.

Menu: There's only the one-player game.

Scoring: Lolo acquires weapons, not points. There's no time limit.

Beginner's Strategy: Here, room by room, is how to get through the first four floors.

Floor 1, room 1: go right, to the heart, shoot the monster and boot it aside, get the top Heart, and go to the Chest.

Floor 1, room 2: Go to the Hearts on the left bottom, left top, right top, and right bottom. When you have them, push the Emerald to the left to protect yourself from Gol's fire—

timing your move to avoid the fire from the Don Medusa above. Go to the open Chest.

Floor 1, room 3: Get the Heart left/center, shoot the monster and boot away the Egg, and get the other Heart in the center. Go counterclockwise around the perimeter to get the rest of the Hearts. If a monster pursues, use the two Bridges on the left side to circumvent and/or confuse it.

Floor 1, room 4: Get the two Hearts on the left side. Go to the right side; push the top and bottom Emeralds to the left, then push the center one down. Shoot the monster and push it to the left to get the 3 Hearts. Hurry back along the top of the maze to the Chest.

Floor 1, room 5: Go to the small room on the bottom left, then to the bottom right, then to the top left. Push the Emerald there to the right as you go to the room on the top right, so you can block the monster.

Floor 2, room 1: Go left, get the bottom-most of the Hearts. That will lure the monster over. (If you stay to get the second Heart now, the monster will get you!) Push the bottom Emerald down to block the passage there, then run to the top and use the Emerald there to imprison the monster. Collect the Hearts at your leisure. *Or* you can try to outrace the evil guardian, getting all the Hearts in a clockwise sweep of the perimeter.

Floor 2, room 2: Go right to the center Emeralds, and block the stationary monsters above using two Emeralds each (that is, blocking the left monster bottom and right, the right monster on the bottom and left). Get all the Hearts.

Floor 2, room 3: Go to the chest: push the Emerald on either side of it one space over. Get the Hearts on the bottom and on the sides. Go back under the Emeralds. When the creature is on the right, push up the Emerald on the left. Ditto the other side. Then go up far left and far right to get the remaining Hearts.

Floor 2, room 4: Get the Heart on the left, then the two on the bottom. Get the Heart top/left, then the one top/right; this will give you the Hammer. Get the Heart in the center, using the Hammer on the Boulder. Hit Snakey with two shots, booting it away, so you can get the Heart.

Floor 2, room 5: The first One-Way Arrow appears here. Get the two Hearts on top. Shoot Snakey and use the Egg to cross the river by going down the right side, just shy of the shore. Shoot the Alma inside, get the Heart, and use the Alma Egg to recross the river. You have a One-Way Pass now; use it to enter the stone chamber on the far right. Get the Heart there and push the third Emerald from the bottom to enter the room to the left. Get the Heart and quickly push the Emerald onto the One-Way Arrow to block the Skulls, which will now attack. When the Skulls have milled away, push the Emerald out and hurry to the Chest.

Floor 3, room 1: Get the Heart directly above you. Turn Snakey into an Egg and push it up to block Medusa. Get the four Hearts above—

one of which will arm you with a Bridge. Cross the river in the center, next to the Emerald. Push the Emerald over the Bridge to the right, next to Snakey. Go under and push the Emerald up, to block the Medusa (sit it right next to her). Go back over the Bridge to the left, get the other lower Emerald, and push it over to block the Medusa from shooting down at you. Go back over the Bridge and get the Hearts on the left. Take the Emerald on top and cross the Bridge to the right. Block the top Medusa so you'll be able to go to the Chest when it's time. Get the Heart on the lower right and race to the Chest before the Skulls cross over.

Floor 3, room 2: Get the Heart above you. Shoot the Alma as it passes under the left Boulder, and use it to cross the River—pushing it up so it's to the left of the Boulder and to the right of the bend in the River. Get the Heart, then catch the Alma Egg as it floats by and ride it back across (if you mess this up, you can shoot the Snakey and use its Egg, if you have to. That, however, will leave you shotless). Go to the top, head right, get the last Heart, then race to the Chest as the monsters come to life.

Floor 3, room 3: Go to the Heart in the center/right and continue in a counterclockwise direction. Use the top/left clump of Boulders (they're in a backward L shape) to elude the Leeper as necessary—or put it to sleep by touching it.

Floor 3, room 4: Push the upper-right Emerald all the way to the lower-right corner. Go around it, to the left. Move left, getting the Hearts there, then head up on the left, go across the top to the right, and get all the Hearts. Go left, travel down the left side, and make your way to the right, to the Chest.

Floor 3, room 5: Clear out the Hearts, except for the one on the bottom right. Move the Emerald on top of Medusa at the very bottom, right beneath the last remaining Heart. Go back around to the right and get the Heart, then head for the Chest.

Floor 4, room 1: Move the second Emerald from the bottom, on the left, to the left when the monster is near the Boulder above. Trap it between the Emerald and the Boulder. Get all the Hearts on the left, then use two Emeralds to box in the monster utterly, bottom and right. Go right; trap the monster there by pushing down the leftmost Emerald when Medusa is next to the Boulders on the left. Get the Hearts, then use the remaining Emeralds to close in the top of the monster—but only when the monster is to the left. Otherwise, it'll zonk you. Repeat this procedure upper right and left.

Floor 4, room 2: Get the bottom Hearts, except for the one above Snakey. Go to the top left. Shoot Snakey and ride the Egg down to the island on the right. Get the Heart fast, hitch a ride on the Snakey Egg to the left island (Snakey will float down the middle). Get the Heart, then return to the Egg *pronto* and float to the bottom. Get the Heart, shoot the Snakey there, and boot it away.

Floor 4, room 3: Push Emerald above so it's to the right of the Boulder that is to the right of the Skull. Go to the far left passage; push the Emerald there under the Skull. Don't get the Heart, yet. Go to the Emerald under the Skull and push up until the Skull is crammed against the top. Go to the upper right; use two blocks top and bottom to block the top and bottom monsters. Use the middle Emerald to jam in the monster on the bottom. Push the last Emerald on the right under Don Medusa in the center, right. Go and get the Heart.

Floor 4, room 4: Move the Emerald above you to the right, until it hits the Tree. Go to the lower right and get the Heart. Push the Emerald to the Bridge; stay under it (so Don Medusa can't blast you), and push it across. Line the Emerald up with the two Trees on top (the Emerald being on the right) and get the Heart. Use the Emerald to trap Don Medusa in the upper-right corner. Get the Heart over the skull. This earns you a Bridge; use it to go over the River to get the heart in the bottom left. Shoot the Gol to the right *fast,* and get to the Chest.

Floor 4, room 5: Go up on the right, push the left-most Emerald there up to block Don Medusa, and get the Heart in the upper right. Go to the Snakeys on the bottom right. Turn the one under the Boulder into an Egg and use it to block the fire from one of the monsters above. Eggify the second Snakey and position it beneath the other monster. Get the Heart in the middle, then repeat the process on the left side.

If you have trouble with any of the above, here are the codes to take you directly to selected higher floors: BKBL to floor 2, room 2; BPBH to floor 2, room 5; BQBG to floor 3, room 1; BYZZ to floor 3, room 5; BZZY to floor 4, room 2; CCZT to floor 4, room 3; and CGZQ to floor 4, room 5.

Advanced Strategy: The following are the strategies for floors 5 and 6:

Floor 5, room 1: Move the second Emerald from the top to the right, and the same with the fourth Emerald from the top. Move the third Emerald from the top *up*, and get the Heart. Move to the right, repeating this maneuver. Move the Emeralds to get to the door.

Floor 5, room 2: Get the Heart on the left, then the one top/left of Medusa (*not* the Heart on the top directly over it). Snatch the Heart on the far left, center (passing to the right under the Boulder, to protect you from the Medusa above). Go to the Emerald to the bottom/right of the right-most Snakey. Push it to the bottom, then go around and push the Emerald on the right to the left, over the other Emerald. Push the bottom Emerald all the way to the left. Gather the three Hearts. Use the Emerald overhead, on the right, to block Medusa on top. Get the Heart there. Go back to the bottom, to the Emerald next to the One-Way Arrow. Push it to the right of Medusa so you can get the Chest.

Floor 5, room 3: Go down the left side, shooting and booting Snakeys and getting the Hearts. When you shoot the last Snakey, don't boot it, just get the Heart. Go to the right, pushing the Emerald all the way up to block Medusa. Get the Heart under Don Medusa and go back to the left to get the remaining Hearts.

Floor 5, room 4: Take the Bridge to the bottom. Go up to the center, then right and up to the cluster of Hearts there. Get the one on the lower right of the pack; this will give you shooting-power. Go to the center left and blow away a Snakey to get to the Heart. Turn a Snakey into an Egg and float down to get the Heart on the bottom left, then float back up before it becomes a snake again. Go up to where you started and use your Bridge power to go back to the cluster of Hearts. Push Emeralds around so you can get the Hearts—all but the two on top. Go all the way down, then to the lower right. Boot the Skull and get the Heart there, then go up to the top right. Use the Bridge to get the Heart there. Now—go to the one Heart in the center, get it, and flee!

Floor 5, room 5: Go left, to the Arrows, then down, right, up, and take a hard right to the right wall. Push the Emerald down to the Boulder. Go left, down, left, and get the Heart. Put the Emerald to the right of Medusa; go back down, then left, and up under the Emerald on the left. Go down and get the Heart.

Stop to the right of the Arrow on the left. Go up, left to the Emerald, and push it all the way to the Boulder on top. Get Hearts there, then go to the right-pointing Arrow on top. Go down to the down-pointing Arrow, then right, up, and get the Heart on top. Go to the top of the Emerald you put beside Medusa. Push the Emerald on your right *to* the right; go down. Go right (under the Emerald), push it to the top, and get the last Heart.

Floor 6, room 1: Use Emeralds thusly: put the one nearest you under the central Medusa, one each over the Medusas on the sides/bottom, and one each next to Medusas on the left and right, center. Go up to the room of Emeralds on the right (using the Hearts to protect you from the Medusas), push up the Emerald over the upper-right corner of the Heart. Skip the next one and push up the Emerald on the far right, then shove the remaining, central Emerald to the right. Go up and get Hearts. Repeat this procedure on the other side (again, using the Hearts as Medusa-blockers), pushing the central Emerald to the left. Reap the Hearts. Go back to the right, to the Emerald that's standing alone on top (the one situated to the bottom/left of the door). Push it between Medusa and the Heart to its right. Repeat on the other side. Go to the Emerald over the last remaining Heart and block the Medusa on the top (between it and the Chest). Collect the Hearts, free of Medusaic interference!

Floor 6, room 2: Get the Heart on top. Go left,

push the Emerald on the right all the way
down, to the left of Medusa. Push the Emerald
beside it up, and get to the left of it. Push it
over the Medusas so it's between them, blocking their horrid gaze. Head left/bottom; push
the Emerald far left down, then the one far
right down. Push the center one over and get
the Hearts. Shoot the top Snakey and push
over Medusa; get the three Hearts on top/
right. Go to the Emerald on top, push it to the
right of the two Medusas on the bottom, and
you're home free.

Floor 6, room 3: This one's a corker. Go to
the right of the Emerald dead center and maneuver it to the right of the Medusa in the
lower right of the screen. Get the Hearts top
right, push the Emerald into the stone chamber—but not so much that you can't get on top
of it to push it back down. Let the Leeper out
of the room . . . following you to the Medusa
in the upper left. Lure it (this will take some
practice) so you can put it to sleep between
the monster and the Heart. Go back and get
the Emerald in the upper-right chamber. Use
it to block the left side of the Medusa in the
center.

Here are some codes to the higher level
rooms: CJZM to floor 5, room 2; CLZK to floor
5, room 4; CMZJ to floor 5, room 5; CPZH to
floor 6, room 1; CRZD to floor 6, room 3. If
you're feeling really daring, punch in CZYY to
heft yourself up to floor 7.

If you really want to have some fun (if suf-
fering is your idea of fun!), punch in DVYB.

You'll go to floor 10 . . . and a confrontation with the Devil himself!

Par: An average player will be clearing four floors in no time flat. A very good player will find floor 6, room 3, the first real challenge.

Training Tips: Since none of the monsters move until you do, and since there's no clock running, study each screen and plan your strategies before you start!

Rating: This is a *wonderful* family game, with challenges for every age group. Shoot-'em-up or action fans will find little to thrill them, however.
  Challenge: B
  Graphics: B—
  Sound Effects: B—

CHAPTER THREE

AMAGON

Type: Fantasy shoot-'em-up.

Manufacturer: American Sammy Corporation, under license from Nintendo.

Objective: Marine hero Amagon is sent to a South Pacific island to investigate sightings of monsters. Armed with a machine gun and possessing the ability to transform himself into the giant Megagon, the bold fighter crash lands on the island. Still, he's determined to explore every inch of the place and make it safely to the rescue ship.

Layout: The screen scrolls horizontally. There are six different zones on the island, with two levels in each.

Hero: Amagon begins the game with 300 Bullets in his gun; when his gun runs dry, he can use the weapon as a club. Upon becoming Megagon, the hero has the ability to throw a powerful Megapunch and fire a Laser Beam.

(However, he can't remain Megagon from level to level, even within each zone.) In addition to being hurt by monsters, Amagon will die if he falls into a River or Valley. When certain monsters are slain, they reward the hero with bonus points: Bullets, a 1-Up, or the Mega-key, without which Amagon can't transform into Megagon. These items remain on the screen for just under 5 seconds, so get to them quickly!

Enemies: There are 43 different monsters. These are outlined in the instruction booklet and are also discussed below. Be aware of the fact that if a monster has fired at you, then dies, its projectiles don't disappear.

Menu: The game is for one player only.

Scoring: Amagon scores points for killing monsters and grabbing bonus "Crowns." When he transforms to Megagon, these points are translated to Mega-points; these are drained when he is hit by a monster, or uses the Laser Beam. Run out of Mega-points as Megagon, and say hello again to Amagon.

Beginner's Strategy: When you start in 1/1, don't waste Bullets on Mushrooms. They take three hits to destroy and don't reward you a proportionate number of points. Just jump them and/or slide under them the first time you encounter the hopping toadstools. The Birds won't trouble you much initially, even though they fire "Eggs" that fly off in three directions. Simply stop when they fire, fine-tune your position as the Eggs fall, and then move on. Or, if you're quick, you can jump up and plug them the instant they flutter in from the right. You'll find your first Mega-key in the sixth tree (the one immediately following the columns in the water). While you cross these columns, pause on the fifth and shoot the Bird; if you leap blindly ahead, the Bird will kill you. When you reach the row of mountains, pause beneath the second from the left. Birds will attack from the right and Snakes from the left. Their assault is staggered, so you can turn from side to side, gunning them all down for points and Crowns (which add 10,000 points). You can obtain up to 6 Crowns this way! By this time you should have over 110,000 points; time to become Megagon. Beat your way to the end of the level, then fight the Lion Man who shows up at the black mountain; he won't be much of a challenge.

Level 1/2 opens with a Mushroom which gives you your next Mega-key. If you make the transformation now, it'll help you with the difficult Birds that lie ahead. If you're not Megagon, there's a 1-Up you can acquire: after you go island-hopping for the second time, go to the first tree for an extra life. In either guise, collect energy for the showdown that lies ahead; after you beat the two Lion Men, you'll face the Lion Head. This appears on the right, facing you. Leap the Fireballs it spits and get in shots immediately; after a few seconds it sprouts a second head on its right side, which also spews Fireballs. The doubleheader will rise; what you must do is slide beneath it, leap up and fire into one face, slide beneath it, leap up and fire into the other face, and repeat the process until it dies.

Level 2/1 presents a new foe: the Elephant Man. When the level begins, crouch and fire at the pachyderm in order to get a Mega-key. Just make sure to keep your arm down when you crouch as Megaman: although Bullets will pass over you, they can hit your arm and kill you. Mosquitoes will buzz in, but if you don't feel like fighting them, simply stand still and they'll go away. If you're still Amagon, shoot them: you'll replenish your Bullet supply relatively easily. After the first Turtle, wait before leaping onto the columns: Moles will attack and must be shot before you continue. When you come to a herd of Elephant Men, you can fight them . . . or take to the treetops and proceed in the branches. When you reach the next Flying Turtle, take a ride on it, then transfer to another when it appears. However, don't make the transfer as soon as the second Turtle flies over: the gap is too great. Wait until it starts to go away then suddenly returns, then make the leap. Birds will attack while you're headed right on the Turtle's back; leap up to avoid their fire (carefully, though; you have to make a slightly forward jump in order to come back down on the Turtle's back). When you come to the Elephant Men, you can fight them by staying on one side of the screen till they approach, then leaping to the other and resuming fire, or you can stay in the tree branches and they'll soon wander off.

At the start of level 2/2, jump up and shoot the Bees; you can use the tree stumps for protection from their projectiles. If you crouch low beside one, hugging it, the Bee ejecta usually won't touch you. You will pass in front of low cliffs, and can walk on the ground or on top of them. Stay on the ground and wait at the end of the last one to shoot the Moles hopping up and the Frogs dropping down. Don't move ahead until they're cleared away. When you come upon the Elephant Men, again, take to the trees—except for the first Elephant Man, who will give you a Mega-key. As for the Turtles, upon reaching the first one, don't get on. Pass under it, shooting the wildlife. It's safer than trying to get them from on Turtle-back. (On the other hand, Turtle riding is like a paid vacation. If you stay on their backs, Mosquitoes will fly under you, and other animals, too, will avoid you.) When you reach the second row of cliffs (where you can walk on the ground or atop the cliffs), stay on the top this time to avoid the Elephant Men at the end . . . unless you have the firepower to deal with them. The boss of this zone is the Devil Tree. It approaches from the right and spits Vampire Bats from its mouth. If you are Megagon, a few Laser Blasts will destroy it, no problem. If you're Amagon, you'll have to leap up and shoot out its eyes. This will take a lot of shooting, during which time you'll have to run from one side of the creature to the other, to keep from being cornered as it shambles across the screen.

Advanced Strategy: The third zone is the River. A general note: when you come to the columns that cross water, you can shoot through the larger ones; that is, crouch behind them and still hit your targets beyond.

After jumping the three narrow pits at the beginning, land on the ledge, crouch at the very left, and fire at once; three Alligator Men will be coming at you from the right. Watch for Snails coming at you from the left as you move on. When you reach a high cliff early on with a sentry Crayfish on the other side, leap off, then duck at once so the animal will leap over you. When you climb onto the floating Log, shoot both left and right to kill the sea life that will leap up at you. After killing the next Alligator Man, you'll get a 1-Up. You'll acquire the Mega-key right after that. As Megaman, you can put the Alligator Men away with just two punches each (though you have to duck to avoid whatever reptile stuff it is they're spitting). Upon reaching the Waterfall, leap onto the second rock from the left, then turn and shoot the Snail that drops toward the first rock. Continue slowly shooting the rest of the falling Snails. Two easy Log rides follow, culminating in a showdown with two easy-to-defeat Alligator Men.

Level 3/2 is the one of the two you'll see if you let the title screen run on without pushing Start (level 1/1 is the other scene on display).

When you start as Amagon, ride the Logs in the ducking mode; you can still shoot whatever comes from the water and collect bonuses, but you'll be a much smaller target. You'll get a Mega-key from the second Alligator Man, though you'd be wise to refrain from becoming Megaman as long as possible, and build up your power; you'll need your strength for the battle with the Hippo Demon at the end of this level. The Hippo Demon is a big, purple lout who hovers in the sky. To reach it, climb the floating rocks at the Waterfall. Its eyes will appear first; don't waste your shots now, since the Hipster is invulnerable in this form. Just avoid the puffs of Hippo-breath, wait till the creature is fully materialized, then dematerialize it with your fire. (Make sure, by the way, that you use Lasers against the Elephant Men you'll meet when you're Megagon. You'll occasionally be rewarded with 1-Ups.)

You're now at level 4/1, and the good news here is that if you die, at least you won't have to continue the game all the way back at the beginning. You "only" get dropped two levels back. As you cross the Forest, Spirits will fly at you from the right. Shoot the first ones for Bullets, watching out for Rats, which may run at you from the left. Jump the Pits, keeping an eye peeled for the Red and Blue Devils which will be hiding behind ledges, spitting all kinds of wicked stuff at you that have a reach of up to half the screen length. They can also

jump up, these gross little heads can, so be
ready to plug 'em.

Fire Balls come at you next, in a "U"-shaped
arc. These are followed by Rats which swarm
from the left and right, while Blue Devils leap
down at you from above. This is a tough region, and you're advised to stay up in the trees
as much as possible. When you're on the
ground, beware the Owls, which come down
at you like feathered yo-yos. You're advised to
jump up and shoot them in the treetops before
they descend.

Your next challenge, 4/2, gives you a 1-Up
almost immediately. Fire Balls rise from the
Pits, so jump the chasms with care. Owls also
descend from the darkness above: keep a
sharp eye out for their glowing eyes. Unfortunately, you can't shoot them while they're in
the dark. If you don't want to risk fighting
them (and collecting goodies), just run past
them quickly, and they won't bother you. This
isn't advisable, however, since you *will* need
Bullets about now.

You'll find three 1-Ups immediately after
the Owl region, followed by Red Devils who
move in a millipede-like chain. Last up is the
Skeleton. Shoot the body. The head will sur-
vive, but it's pretty easy to punch out.

Frightful 5/1 begins with Dragon Birds and
Armadillos, depending on whether you hit the
high or low trail. In any event, you'll get a
1-Up from either. When you reach the second
Cloud, go under it, to the right, to lure out the
Dragon Bird. Kill it and jump left to get on top

of the Cloud. Run through the Triceratops skull (no danger here). When you cross the cliff wall, be careful: Blocks four, seven, and ten will fall out from under you if you tarry. So . . . cross fast! All the Blue Dinosaurs you'll encounter immediately thereafter will give you Bullets, while the Clouds presage a Pterodactyl attactyl. Stay on the Clouds and duck so the dinobirds won't get you. When you finally reach the monstrous Megasaurus, duck its fireballs and shoot at its horn. It's surprisingly simple to slay.

The sixth and final zone is more of the same. Lobsters will try to climb trees and jump down at you; shoot them before they reach the top, and you'll be okay. As for the Alien who runs the show, the skirt-wearing extraterrestrial can only be destroyed by blasting the small silvery star which orbits it. Not easy, especially since the titanic figure will be shooting energy balls at you. But hey! You're Amagon, and it's only a matter of time before you triumph!

Par: A good player will be able to clear the first two zones completely. Things begin to head up in 2/2 . . . but you should have stored enough lives and energy to get through.

Training Tips: Watch the sample screens that appear after the title screen. These will let you know what kind of foes are in store in the first and third zones. Also, practice going through the levels as Amagon instead of Megagon. It'll harden you as a fighter!

Rating: Reminiscent of *Adventure Island,* the game is actually more interesting if you play as Amagon than as the too-powerful Megagon. In any case, there's something to entertain everyone here.

Challenge: B+

Graphics: B+ (good animation, and mesmerizing water graphics in zone three)

Sound Effects: B—

CHAPTER FOUR

BAD DUDES

Type: Martial arts bash-'em-up.

Manufacturer: Data East, under license from Nintendo.

Objective: The vile Dragon Ninja has kidnapped the President, and it's up to you to get to his helicopter before the criminal overlord can get away. But that's no easy task, as you pit your martial arts skills against a wave of weapon-toting enemies.

Layout: The screen scrolls horizontally, with occasional vertical motion. There are seven different levels.

Hero: A Bad Dude is a fighter who can move from side to side, duck, or face upward, and can punch or kick in any of those directions. He can also gather power-up objects he finds along the way; these are described below and in the instruction booklet. One tactic that is *not* described is the "power punch." If you hold down the A button (with Turbo off, if you're using the NES Advantage), you can do a super-powerful punch. The only drawback is that it takes slightly more time to execute, which can be dangerous when the timer is low.

Enemies: You'll face nine different types of warrior; these are described in the instruction booklet. The toughest are the Super Warriors, who appear at the end of each level.

Menu: One or two players can be a Bad Dude, though on alternate turns only.

Scoring: You earn points for defeating a foe and finishing a level. The breakdown is described in the instruction booklet. You also race against a timer.

Beginner's Strategy: Because each level is more or less the same, there aren't as many strategies in this game as in other martial arts games.

The City: You've got forty timer-seconds (longer than real seconds) to clear this level. The Blue and White Ninjas are killed with kicks or punches. Stay on the Fence and Truck top as much as possible; you can see the guys down below before they jump up at you, and can position yourself accordingly. If you're below, your enemies can jump down on you; the last thing you want is to have them fall on your head while tossing deadly Stars (which is what the White and Red Ninjas throw). If you're hit by a Star, or even touch one that's on the ground, you lose power. To avoid these, leap up, don't duck. You can also leap to the ground and back up to the Fence, or vice versa. Lady Ninjas and Samurais also occasionally attack here, the latter leaping over you. Let them do so, then turn and hit them when they're behind you. Another very effective strategy is to wait for any foe to leap up onto the Fence. As soon as it jumps you, jump down. The Ninja will come right down again, in the same place from which he or she first jumped. Knowing this, you can clobber her or him on his way down. The level's Super Warrior arrives at approximately the 28-second mark (give or take a few seconds, depending upon whether you stayed to fight everyone that attacked or moved on, fighting only when you had to). Punch him, then jump onto the Fence to avoid his fire. He'll jump up, at which point you can hit him again; jump down again, and he'll follow. Repeat as often as it takes to kill him.

The Big Rig: You have 60 seconds to clear this screen as you fight Ninjas on the top of a Truck. Take care not to fall off: you lose power every instant you're on the ground. Also, avoid going to the extreme left or right of the screen. Ninjas will throw their stars before they arrive on the screen; you'll be hit before you can duck or beat the enemy. The screen will scroll slowly toward the left, revealing the front of the Truck. You'll obtain the Knife from one of the Ninjas up here, along with at least one Energy tin (two, if you've killed the right Ninjas). When the Cab finally scrolls into view, jump down and duck right in front of the grill. Punch left and right with the Knife, killing Ninjas. A Super Warrior will attack now; he's a squat little terror with claws. Just duck these and punch him; you can declaw him without too much effort.

The Sewer: This level is a 50-second exercise. The other thing to watch out for here are the open Drains: if you step in front of them, you'll lose power. As in level one, stay on the top tier of the sewer as much as possible. The boss of this level will appear at approximately the 35-second mark. When you're at the far right, the Super Warrior will fall on you; rush to the left, on the top level. This guy's going to start splitting, becoming two pairs of Ninjas. Using the Knife or Nunchucks you obtained from the Red Ninja shortly before, kill the first pair that rushes you, then meet the second pair. The original Ninja will attack and then split again, so stand your ground and repeat what you just did. This will happen a total of three or four times, depending upon how quickly you were able to defeat the Super Warrior. If at any time the last Ninja divides on the top level, jump to the bottom and make your stand there.

Advanced Strategy:

The Forest: This is a 70-second level. Stay on the top cliff and kick the Dog who attacks. After the two-level cliff, you'll be on the ground. A Flaming Ninja will attack: stand and fight using a kick (or jump him and let him run on, if you don't care about the points). In a moment the screen will scroll vertically, so you can move down. At the Tree Stump the dead Ninja usually leaves behind Nunchucks. The screen will soon scroll vertically once more. When it does and you continue to the right, stay on the top level. The boss will arrive at roughly the 40-second mark. Go to the far right and begin punching (with the Knife, preferably) as soon as the Super Warrior's energy bar appears. You'll get in a few licks before he can squeeze fully onto the screen. Shift at once to the left to avoid his kick, then resume knifing him.

The Freight Train: You have 70 seconds to clear this one. The best strategy is basically to stand still on top of the Southern & Pacific train, letting the enemy come to you and making only slight adjustments as the screen scrolls slowly to the right. You usually get Nunchucks shortly after the Flaming Ninja shows up. At the beginning of the blue car, one of your victims usually deposits a Clock, which adds time. (If it falls off, though, don't bother to get it. It's not *that* beneficial on this level.) The Super Warrior arrives at approximately 29 seconds, at the end of the blue car. He'll be swinging a ball and chain, which is quite deadly. Go to the far left as soon as his energy bar appears. When he swings his weapon, use your jumpkick to come up *under* it and nail him.

. The last remaining levels, *The Cave* and *The Factory,* offer the same challenges, as well as a few new ones: falling Stalactites in the Cave (just keep your eyes on the ceiling and be prepared to dodge the rock spikes), and the Super Warriors in the Factory, who you should fight as before. When you reach the Factory and the Dragon Ninja tries to make a getaway in his chopper, move quickly: if you don't get onto the runner, everything will be for naught!

Par: A good player's cumulative point breakdown: 14,000 after level one; 40,000 after two; 85,000 after three; 130,000 after four; 180,000 after five; 225,000 after six; and 270,000 at game's end.

Training Tips: As in all fighting games, learn how to work your warrior with precision. One kind of demented exercise you might want to try is playing both Bad Dudes . . . by yourself! Work each, using only the buttons, and see how that improves your concentration when you go back to playing with one. Or you can skip that, and start the game with over sixty lives! During the title screen, hit B, A, down, up, down, up on controller two, then Start on controller one. You will then be, truly, a seriously bad dude!

Rating: The fighting is fun, and the choice of weapons provides some variety. Overall, though, there's a sameness to the levels, which makes this one, ultimately, a disappointment.

   Challenge: C
   Graphics: B+ (excellent scenery)
   Sound Effects: B—

CHAPTER FIVE

BLADES OF STEEL

Type: Hockey game.

Manufacturer: Konami, under license from Nintendo.

Objective: Scoring as many goals as possible, and protecting your own goal during three periods of play.

Layout: During regular play the view is from the bleachers as two teams face off. During penalty shots the view is from over the shooting player's shoulder.

Hero: Your players skate, pass or shoot the Puck using a Stick, and also punch during fights. You can also ram an opposing player to free the puck; one to three collisions in a row usually does it. Your goalie slides from side to side to protect the goal.

Enemies: Same as *Hero.* When the computer controls the opposing team, there's no faking the players out.

Menu: Two players can skate against each other, or one can battle the Stanley Cup–caliber computer.

Scoring: You earn a point whenever you knock the Puck into your opponent's goal. Your team suffers a timed penalty—a player is removed from the ice—for icing, slashing, and checking, as outlined in the instruction booklet; he's also penalized for losing a fight (the winner is not punished).

Beginner's Strategy: To begin the game, at the face-off hit the B button repeatedly and pull the joystick down toward the player nearest you. Most of the time you'll get the Puck to him (provided your opponent doesn't try this strategy as well). Vary the following two moves to keep your opponent on his or her toes. When the player nearest you gets the Puck, race to the opposite side of the rink, then skate along the boards and cut in just shy of the goal. Your opponent usually won't be able to get to you because of the cluster of players at center ice following the face-off. (This move also works best against the computer. It immediately gives chase to the player with the Puck, which leaves fewer men between you and the goal.) When this maneuver threatens to become predictable, get the puck to the player nearest you, and instead of going all the way up, cut toward the goal as soon as you reach the center circle. This latter quick, aggressive maneuver will often catch the other player off guard. As long as you switch between these two moves, the other player will never be sure which one you'll use.

If this tactic doesn't result in a goal, you'll be playing across the full ice. Above all, use passes—especially if all of your opponent's players are clustered around your goal, and you need to get the Puck across the ice in a hurry. The time not to pass, obviously, is if you're surrounded by your opponent's men. In that case, show them your back and try to skate out. Or skate behind the cage and use it for protection (stopping short and coming out the way you entered is a good fake-out). Use your own men for a "pick" if necessary, skating around them while they block your foes.

At the goal get in close and take repeated shots. Most players find this the best way to score. However, there are players who swear by the long-shot technique: shooting from their own territory. One of your players is almost always near enough to your opponent's goal to intercept the shot and slap it in. The danger of this is twofold: if the opposing goalie catches the slow-moving shot, you've lost the Puck; and if your shot goes wide of the goal, you'll be hit with an icing penalty.

Advanced Strategy: In any game against the computer, there's only one strategy: speed! At the most difficult level you'll barely have time to think—which can be dangerous, since the computer will intercept anything but a perfect pass. Moreover, it can't be disoriented by fancy passing. At best, it will only be a step behind you, which means that if you slow down or hold the Puck too long, it's going to block or steal. Keep your players and the Puck moving! As for scoring, you can usually assume your first shot's going to be blocked: the computer has enough time to position the goalie to block you. What works best is hitting the goal hard, recovering your own missed shot, and striking again fast. If you can manage this attack from the center of the cage, so much the better; you can quickly jockey up or down and slip the Puck in the sides.

Par: Even Bobby Orr would be lucky to earn a tie against the computer at its most difficult level.

Training Tips: Needless to say, the best training you can receive is to play the computer at its top proficiency level.

Rating: A brilliant re-creation of hockey, and quite possibly the best game for two players. Watch for the mini-games you sometimes get to play between periods. Though they're shameless plugs for other Konami games, it was an inspired idea to put them there!
Challenge: A
Graphics: B+
Sound Effects: B+

CHAPTER SIX

THE BUGS BUNNY CRAZY CASTLE

Type: Maze-type chase.

Manufacturer: Kemco-Seika, under license from Nintendo.

Objective: Bugs's girlfriend, Honey Bunny, has been captured by Daffy Duck, Sylvester, Wiley Coyote, and Yosemite Sam, and imprisoned somewhere in a castle. Bugs must find her, collecting Carrots for energy while disabling and/or avoiding his foes. Bugs can't proceed to the next room until he's gathered all the Carrots on each level.

Layout: The characters move in all directions, across screens showing Ladders and platforms, as well as Pipes and Doorways for rapid transport around the screen. The picture scrolls horizontally or vertically, depending upon the level. There are sixty levels in all.

Hero: Bugs can walk and climb stairs. He can also find the power-up items: Magic Carrot Juice (for invisibility and invincibility, which lasts a whole, big five seconds); and a Boxing Glove (to punch an enemy insensible from a distance). The glove can be reclaimed if it hasn't struck anyone. Safes, Wooden Crates, Buckets, and Ten Ton Weights are also available to drop on opponents or simply to shove against them. (Both techniques work. However, objects cannot be left atop Pipes or in front of Doorways to block foes: they'll walk right through them.) You can walk safely over a foe who's been clobbered. Bugs starts with five lives and loses them during play, or gains them when he beats a bonus screen (see *Enemies*).

Enemies: Your enemies can be very diligent when it comes to guarding Carrots; they just won't leave, unless you lure them away by wandering off. And if you touch them, you die. However, once they do go, they can't always find their way back. Another good thing about them: you can pass them inside a Doorway or Pipe without being hurt. It's too dark in there for them to find you! In addition to your foes—whose touch will cost you a life—watch out for the No Carrot sign. Touch it, and you'll get bounced into a special level, a riotous maze of Pipes. If you lose here, you'll go back three screens. (If you win, though, you earn three extra lives.)

Menu: There's only the one-player game.

Scoring: Points are awarded for each foe clobbered and Carrot obtained (there are no points for Boxing Gloves). Carrots are 100 points on all levels; your foes are also always the same, ranging from 100 to 1000 points (the latter, for a Wooden Crate dropped off a top floor onto Sylvester, for example).

Beginner's Strategy: The screens are self-explanatory, and, for the most part, no "one way" is best to beat them. Thus, here are some basic tips and landmarks, as well as the passwords that will bring you to every level of the game.

Level 3: Outwait them on the left, climb, and push the Crate on your foes.

Level 7: This is the first Pipe level.

Level 8: In order to get certain Carrots, you need to do some fancy footwork. On the left side of the screen, for example, go to the lowest Pipe on the bottom, zoom up, and drop off the ledge on top to get the left Carrot; you'll nab it on your fall down. Go up the Pipe on the second level and drop off the ledge for the right Carrot.

Level 10: Get the left Glove first, then the right one.

The passwords:

1. *Just turn the game on!*	6. SXES
2. SZWS	7. ZW4S
3. ZS2S	8. ZX95
4. ZZPS	9. WSRS
5. SW3S	10. WZFS

11. XSJS	21. SP3Z
12. XZKS	22. SYEZ
13. WWMS	23. ZP4Z
14. WXCS	24. ZY9Z
15. XWAS	25. W2RZ
16. XXOS	26. WTFZ
17. S2SZ	27. X2JZ
18. STWZ	28. XTKZ
19. Z22Z	29. WPMZ
20. ZTPZ	30. WYCZ

Advanced Strategy: A few general tips, then the passwords:

Level 30: The first No Carrots sign appears here.

Level 36: Complete the entire left side first.

Level 45: There's a No Carrots sign on this level.

Level 52: Save your Gloves for the two rooms on the upper right. You'll need them here.

Level 53: Clear the center first, then drop down the right side.

Level 55: Conquer this room from the bottom up.

Level 57: Again, bottom to top.

Level 60: No Carrots sign here.

The passwords:

31. XPAZ	36. TZPW
32. XYOZ	37. 2W3W
33. 2SSW	38. 2XEW
34. 2ZWW	39. TW4W
35. TS2W	40. TX9W

41. PSRW	51. T22X
42. PZFW	52. TTPX
43. YSJW	53. 2P3X
44. YZKW	54. 2YEX
45. PWMW	55. TP4X
46. PXCW	56. TY9X
47. YWAW	57. P2RX
48. YXOW	58. PTFX
49. 22SX	59. Y2JX
50. 2TWX	60. YTKX

Par: Everyone's point score will be roughly the same, since you have to collect all the Carrots before you can move on, and will probably get rid of most of the enemies in order to get to the Carrots! A child should have no trouble getting to level 8, while a more experienced videogamer won't have any serious trouble until level 45.

Training Tips: The most difficult skill to master in this game is beaning your enemies from a high level; you've got to time your push just right, or your target will wander away. Work on this, and also get in some practice on level 60.

Rating: Like *Mickey Mousecapade,* this is an ideal game for the entire family. Though experienced players will find it somewhat simple, the graphics are charming and it's still enjoyable.

    Challenge: B

    Graphics: B+ (The characters are all well-delineated, and the bulge that appears when they shimmy up a Pipe is wonderful!)

Sound Effects: C— (Okay music, but little else . . . most disappointingly, no "What's Up, Doc?")

CHAPTER SEVEN

BUMP 'N' JUMP

Type: Auto race.

Manufacturer: Vic Tokai, under license from Nintendo.

Objective: While you and your girlfriend are out tooling around in your car Popper, the evil Jackals attack. They steal your lady pal, and you set off to rescue her. She reappears every fifth screen, though you can't save her until the very end of the game.

Layout: The view is from overhead as the car drives from the bottom to the top of the screen. The race carries you through four districts, each of which has sixteen courses.

Hero: Your car has the ability to speed up, brake, maneuver from side to side, jump breaks or obstacles in the road, nudge other cars aside by bumping into them, or jump and come down on them, smashing them to scrap metal. As you travel, be alert to pick up Power Barrels (extra fuel)—most of these are located in the same places from game to game—and Bonuses (extra cars). The latter first appears on the third screen of the first level. Also available are (unannounced) Repair bonuses. These are dropped from Trucks, also beginning in the third screen of the first level. Grab one of these and you'll be spirited to a repair shop; while there, keep jabbing the A button and you'll find yourself with more gasoline than a refinery! You can only make leaps when you've reached a speed of 150 km/hour. If your power gauge hits that old goose-egg zero, you can't jump at all.

Enemies: Just as you can nudge other cars away, they can force you aside. The instruction booklet lists the nine different kinds of vehicles you'll face, as well as their weaknesses and strengths. Many of these are discussed below. Not every vehicle appears at once; for example, the Bulldozers don't arrive until 1/4, and the Fuel Trucks won't come unless you follow the "braking start-up" outlined below. The sides of the road and buildings are also enemies: if you hit them, you crack up.

Menu: There's only a one-player game.

Scoring: You earn points for smashing other vehicles; these range from 100 for cars to 500 for trucks. At the end of each round you're awarded 300 extra points for each vehicle you wrecked. If you can land smack on the marker at the end of each screen—for example, the person waving the banner, though not on the flag itself, at the end of 1/2—you'll be awarded an extra 5000 points!

Beginner's Strategy: There are two different, equally valid strategies to use when playing this game. The first is the "braking start-up," which is designed to rack up points by racking up cars. All of the cars enter the picture from the bottom left. Shift there, depress the brake, and you'll cause massive pile-ups behind you. With your finger on the brake, you'll also easily spot and collect the Power Barrels that come along. Accelerate only when you see the "!" warning at the top of the screen (which means there's an obstacle coming up that needs to be jumped). This technique works especially well in the later rounds, when the road curves and splits into narrow paths. You should also brake whenever you come out of a leap over an obstacle. Other vehicles will be landing on the lower left, and it's a good time to cream a bunch. However—creeping along sort of defeats the point of a racing game, so you should use it sparingly. The other technique—the "leapfrog method" —is discussed below. (If you use the braking technique on 1/1, the Fuel Truck will appear instead of the Cement Mixer. They're both equally dangerous.)

When you race normally, there are a few things to watch out for. Nudging cars diagonally (that is, your fender coming up and hitting the left or right of theirs) doesn't guarantee you'll destroy a car. If you hit them into a cranny on the side of the screen, they have a very good chance of bouncing right out again. A better method is to get right beside them and hit them hard to the left or right twice in succession. If you find yourself getting nudged over in this fashion, you can try to fight your way back with bumps of your own—but that doesn't always work. Better to take a diagonal jump and get out of there.

You don't have a lot of room for error when jumping up and landing on a specific car. In order to bean a Truck, for example, you must leap as soon as the front end appears at the bottom of the screen. And you must be racing at top speed. Otherwise, it will come along and pass you before you can make your jump. When you jump up and land on a car, if your own car is perilously close to the side of the road, tug it immediately to the opposite side, so you won't get caught in the crack-up. If you've already jumped up to land on a car, and a "!" flashes, abort your jump by hitting the brake. You *can* try and finish your maneuver, then hit the ground and take off immediately—but if you haven't the speed to make the second jump, you're going to crash. Only experienced Bump 'n' Jumpers should try this.

A final general tip: you can jump on Cement or Fuel Trucks, but if you miss them, all is not lost. Go to the opposite side from where they are and nudge other cars diagonally up into their wake. Crashing another vehicle into a

Truck's obstacle will earn you regular crash points!

Advanced Strategy: The "leapfrog technique" of playing is dangerous, more fun than a barrel of monkey wrenches. This game is played mostly at top speed, and goes thusly.

In 1/1 make the Cement Trucks your primary target. Not only are they rich in points, but when they crash, they usually take one or two other cars with them because of their size. And you get the points. The first Cement Truck comes almost at once, from the bottom left, then every two or three seconds thereafter. Hop from one to the other, pausing only to leap the breaks in the highway.

In 1/2 there are five walls to jump. The first two are well spaced, so you'll have plenty of time to jump on Trucks in the meantime. The last three come in quick succession; don't take time out to smash anything. Just jump, land, jump, land, jump, and brake hard to come to rest on the flag person.

In 1/3 the leapfrog is ideal as you travel through farmland. Position yourself on the left orange center divider and *stay on it!* The road will narrow (the right side disappears) and Trucks will come up behind you. If you keep up a steady leapfrog motion, you'll not only bash the trucks, but you won't be pushed to the side by the other cars in these crowded areas. When the road widens again at intervals, you can dart to the right to pick up Power Barrels. (A word of caution here: if you're an adventurous player, do the leapfrogging but *don't* smash the Trucks. Remember, some of them carry important bonuses. Having said that, weigh the fact that gambling on getting a 1-Up isn't worth losing a life because you crash into a load of cement.) The narrow stretches of road end after a while, and you have to leap sandy oases. These aren't tough, as long as you know they're coming up.

In 1/4, for the first time in the game the roads wind diagonally, and if you leave them, you crash. Worse, there are Boulders and Roadblocks in your way. You can stay on the ground during the short straightaways; otherwise, keep leapfrogging. As you come down from your jump, jiggle the joystick/controller from side to side, fine-tuning your landing to avoid the obstacles below. When the "!" flashes, be prepared to take a mighty leap over the roadless countryside to the end.

Level 1/5 is similar to 1/2 . . . at the start. A short way in you'll find big, fat, intrusive buildings sitting right in the middle of the course, the road forking around them. Experienced racers will be able to leap these (in one giant hop, or two quick hops), or you can go around them left or right. If you want to smash cars, hop the buildings diagonally so you land in the middle of the roads on the sides—ahead of the rest of the traffic. Total the cluster of vehicles that are usually there, then skid around the building and continue on your journey.

By this time you'll have seen virtually all of

the kinds of variations the game throws at you. In later stages the traffic thickens, obstacles are more plentiful, and roads twist more and more. (In other words, you'll *need* a trip or two to the Repair shop.) However, if you've mastered the basic skills to this point, while you won't exactly have an *easy* time ahead, you'll manage to get through many of the levels.

Par: You should be pouncing on or smashing an average of fifteen cars in each screen.

Training Tips: If you've got NES Advantage (and a lot of patience), run through the later courses when you reach them, using slow motion, so you can see the dangers. Otherwise, the most important skill to master is the leap/brake combination, so you can abort a jump if a "!" suddenly looms, or can land on the bonus marker at the end of a screen.

Rating: This cartridge offers many enjoyable variations on the *Spy Hunter* racing theme. The ability to play either a jumping-style or old-fashioned racing game adds to already fine play value.
    Challenge: A
    Graphics: B—
    Sound Effects: B+

CHAPTER EIGHT

BURGER TIME

Type: Chutes and Ladders type climbing game.

Manufacturer: Data East, under license from Nintendo.

Objective: You're Chef Peter Pepper, and you're faced with a screen full of Ladders and Platforms, the latter being covered with Buns, Hamburger Patties, and Lettuce. Your job is to drop them from level to level until a Hamburger has been constructed at the bottom. The only problem is that Food Foes chase you around the screen, and their touch is deadly!

Layout: The screen doesn't scroll at all; the layout of Ladders and Platforms changes each time all the Hamburgers have been constructed. There are six different screens in all.

Hero: Peter has the ability to climb Ladders, run, and sprinkle Pepper, which briefly paralyzes the Food Foes. He can replenish his supply of the seasoning by collecting foods (such as Ice Cream or Coffee) which occasionally appear in the center of the screen. Peter can also drop elements of the Hamburger on top of the Foes to kill them, and/or he can drop elements as the Foes are crossing them behind him, which will also result in their demise.

Enemies: The characters always appear in the same patterns—though their movement after that depends entirely upon what Peter does, since they home in on him. Mr. Hot Dog and Mr. Egg appear from the very start; Mr. Pickle doesn't arrive until the third level.

Menu: One or two players can enjoy the game separately.

Scoring: Peter earns points for killing Food Foes and dropping elements of the Hamburger to lower levels. More points are acquired, and the elements fall lower, if a Food Foe is on top of one when it falls.

Beginner's Strategy: The bad news is there's no way to continue the game or to access different levels other than by plodding through the ones that come before. So, get set for a long haul to reach the end of *Burger Time*. Fortunately, it won't be an unchallenging haul! Also, if you've begun dropping a Hamburger part when you lose one of your five lives, that part will be just as you left it when you return with your next life. Finally, this generalization: if you have to run from Food Foes, or want to lure them away, try to take the longest straightaway you can find. If you get them started on long paths, it'll take them longer to get off, turn around, and come after you again.

In all levels the important thing is to get to the top of the screen and drop items from above. When they fall, they not only push items below them down a level, but they limit the amount of ground you have to cover. As more Food Foes enter the screen, you will be roaming far and wide to lure them away, and then rushing back to drop items. Because of this, you'll want to keep the Hamburger-item area as compact as possible, so you can rush in, do your job, and get away again before the Food Foes arrive. The best way to do this, again, is by tightening the screen by dropping objects from the top to the bottom.

The initial screen is easy enough to beat if you first perform this simple maneuver. Head up the central blue Ladder. On the top level cut to the right and drop the two Bun tops there. Go down the far right ladder, cut left over the Lettuce, go up the next Ladder, and go right. Pause in the center of the Bun until Mr. Hot Dog comes at you from the right, then hit him with a cloud of Pepper and drop the Bun top. It will fall hard and far, nearly completing the Hamburger. Rush down and finish the sandwich, then go to the right, along the bottom. Drop two Patties, then cut up and knit your way to the center, where Ice Cream has just appeared. Collect it for additional Pepper, then head to the top of the screen and start building the Hamburger on the left. The level is pretty easy to clear once you've done this.

Level two is more difficult by far. Begin by racing straight up the center (the Food Foes coming at you from either side won't get to you in time). Although there are several courses you can follow, the best is this one. (Note: while you're being chased across this narrow screen by food, you may panic and forget all about the pattern. If you do, remember: work your way down from the top. There are two dead-end platforms on the bottom, and if you get trapped here while there are still Hamburger elements above, you're going to die on this level.)

Go to the top right and drop the two Buns one level. Descend to the center of the screen and go up the central blue Ladder. Cut across the Pattie and Lettuce near the top on the left, get the Bun on the top left and drop it a level. Climb down the green Ladder beneath it, to the Pattie. Cut right, drop the Pattie, and continue across the Lettuce to the central blue Ladder. Go up the green Ladder to the right and drop the Bun above one level. Cross it the other way and drop it a second level. Go to the last blue Ladder on the right and climb to the top. Go left and drop the Bun all the way to the bottom, using a crisscrossing technique (Mr. Hot Dog will be hot on your apron, so be careful!). Go to the top and come down the central blue Ladder. Drop the Bun on the far right. Start up the blue Ladder on the far right to lure all the Mr. Hot Dogs—then rush back down, cut left, and go up the central blue Ladder to the Bun in the upper left. Drop it, just as Mr. Hot Dog comes waddling on to it. Follow the Bun down, go right, get the Coffee that will appear, and finish the last remaining Hamburger.

Advanced Strategy: On level three there are Hamburgers to be built on top, and also one on the left and one on the right, bottom. At the start of level three a whirling Mr. Pickle comes flying in from the left. Thus, you should head immediately to the right side and begin there. The path you must take is simple: finish the Hamburger on the right, head to the top and drop those, working your way left and right until they're finished, then go to the one on the bottom left. The thing to keep in mind is that even Food Foes who have been slain return after a few seconds, so that by the end of the round you'll have a ton of enemies swarming on a very small space. Though you only have the one Hamburger to assemble on the lower left, it'll often be necessary to go running elsewhere to lead the Food Foes away.

There's no point in giving a more detailed pattern to the remaining three levels: you won't be able to follow one. Food Foes come at you too fast and work to corner you. In general, follow the top to bottom plan, don't allow yourself to get pinned in a corner, and don't be afraid to abandon a piece of Hamburger, even if you're a step away from dropping an element. You'll often escape pursuing Food

Foes by no more than a single step, and it's better to have to return to finish the job than not to be able to return!

Par: Since this is a *tough* game, players needn't feel ashamed if they only get as far as level three.

Training Tips: If you have the NES Advantage, play the game in slow motion. This will allow you to go through all of the screens and study them before you have to play at regular speed.

Rating: There may not be a lot of diversity here, and you're going to be frustrated that there's no "continue" mode . . . but the game is still a pip.

> *Challenge:* A
> *Graphics:* B— (The animation's okay, but the pictures lack detail.)
> *Sound Effects:* C+ (The music's suitably light-hearted, but some sizzly or squooshy food sounds would have been fun.)

CHAPTER NINE

CASTLEVANIA II: SIMON'S QUEST

Type: Fantasy-horror quest.

Manufacturer: Konami, under license from Nintendo.

Objective: You defeated Count Dracula in *Castlevania,* yet you feel like someone's driven a stake through *your* heart. You're in constant pain, and no wonder: you're under Dracula's curse. The only way to lift it is to find his five body parts and burn them in his castle.

Layout: There are six different vistas, all of which scroll from right to left, with minimal vertical play. These same scenes—the Church, the Graveyard, the Forest Primeval, etc.—are to be found as you travel from village to village.

Hero: As Simon Belmont, you can obtain 20 different power-up items as you pick your way through Transylvania. These are detailed in the instruction booklet and are also discussed below. Hearts are the most valuable, since they can be used to buy weapons (see *Scoring*). Keep in mind that once a Heart is exposed, it stays for just 5 seconds before vanishing. Entering a church will also restore your energy. You begin the game with a Leather Whip, which has limited killing ability and reach. Note: you can kill monsters behind Simon while whipping in front. If you let them get near enough, the recoil of your elbow as you snap the lash will destroy them!

Enemies: The instructions illustrate the 24 "Best Buddies" of Dracula you'll be facing. And, of course, there's ol' pointy-teeth himself to dispose of.

Menu: There's only the one-player game.

Scoring: The game has a clock. As time passes, night descends, causing two things to happen: the monsters become twice as difficult to kill (for example, it takes four hits of the Leather Whip to kill Wolf Men, instead of two), and the people you must see to buy weapons go into hiding. You gain or lose energy as you're struck by monsters, fall into lava, etc.; you also collect Hearts, which are left behind by most of the monsters you slay (at night you earn two Hearts per kill instead of one). However, you can't store more than 200 Hearts at a time. If you try, you lose them all (they're transferred to energy, and your energy level is automatically filled to the brim).

Beginner's Strategy: The first thing you have to do is acquire weapons beyond the weak Leather Whip with which you start. But before you set out, keep in mind that you must always attack monsters as they approach. It's the only way you can collect Hearts. If need be, hang around and let monsters cluster so you can collect more—or seek them out in the Forest or Graveyard, as described below.

Go right to the first set of steps. Go down one flight, buy a White Crystal from the shrouded woman, go down another flight and head right. Whip the Wolf Men and skeletal Freddies in the Forest until you have at least 50 Hearts, then go back to the left and up two flights. (If night has fallen, stay and kill Zombies in the village until daybreak. If night falls when you're still in the Forest, fight the Wolf Men by hitting one with your whip, backing up, hitting again, etc. Don't stand still, or it'll pounce on you before you can get four hits in.) At dawn, head down a flight and go right. Buy Holy Water from the first shrouded figure you encounter, then go down a flight and continue right. Fight Wolf Men and Freddies for more Hearts, using the Whip and salvos of Holy Water to expedite the slaughter. When day breaks, go down one flight, go left, jump the pit, and enter the first open door. Buy the Thorn Whip, which is more powerful than your dumb Leather Whip. Go right, into the Forest, and continue right until you reach the River. Fish Men will jump out at you, but one strike of the lash and it's Davy Jones' Locker for them. They have a habit of jumping as you leap from island to island (while you're at the peak of your jump), so be ready to whip them. You shouldn't even have to break your stride.

When you reach the next screen, stay on the top. When you enter the screen after that, climb down the first flight of steps. Continue right, to the new town. Go into the first open door and head to the right wall. Toss Holy Water at the wall, to break it down. There will be a shrouded figure in the next room; buy a Dagger and retrace your steps to the street. Go right, enter the Church to collect energy, then leave and head right. You'll have to jump a lava river and fight Freddies, but that's fine: you can use the Hearts. When the Ghostly Eyeballs descend, simply jump up and whip them before they can begin to pester you. When night falls, Ravens will attack; kill these immediately. After they swoop at you twice, they'll drop down low and come at you like a rocket. (If that happens, jump over them when they zoom toward you.) At dawn go to the open door at the end of town. Use Holy Water to destroy the stone floor on the left side, and descend. There's a woman who'll sell you a Chain Whip for 150 Hearts; buy it. Leave the room and go right toward the lava screen. Stay on the top ledge, head right, and go to the next screen. At the bottom of the steps destroy the two blocks that comprise the bottom step, and go left. Hurl Holy Water on the wall at the end and get the Flame, which weakens your enemies. (It also weakens you, sad to say: you lose a Heart each time you employ it!) Go right, to the Forest, where you'll face Zombies and Spiders—some of whom toss snowflakelike webs that'll slow you down. Continue right, past a set of steps. (Don't descend these, but note where they are.) You'll enter a village; if you need Hearts, continue to the right, into the Graveyard, and kill the Zombie Hands here. When you have at least 100 Hearts, go left to the edge of the village. Climb one flight to the door on the right. Enter, break the center of the floor and descend. Go right into the door and buy Laurels, which will give you invincibility. Return to the Graveyard for more Hearts, then go left, on the bottom, to the door that is to the left of the small gray signpost. (Entering the one on the right is a waste of time.) Smash the floor, go down, and buy Garlic from the woman there. Go up the right side of the room and head left, past the stairs (the ones you were told above to note). Continue past them until you reach the mansion, then go in the first door. Use the White Crystal to see the elevator, which is the only way you can cross the pit. Rise and get off on the solid brick sticking from the wall. Toss Knives at the fiendish Knight to the right; when he perishes, go right to the steps that lead up. Climb, watching out for the Blobs that cling to the floor and flop up at you. Go left and jump up the ledges. Climb the stairs, go right, and stop at the edge of the ledge. See the ledge on the right, slightly higher than you? The two blocks on its left side are fake. When you jump, make sure you land on the third one in, or you'll plummet to your death. Go right, down two flights, head to the next staircase and go down, and continue right to the end of the corridor. Use Holy Water to break the wall and get the Book here. Check your inventory and make sure you have at least 50 Hearts; if not, kill some Zombies and get 'em. Go left, up two flights to the woman, and buy an Oak Stake. Just be careful, here and hereafter, not to touch those grayish spikes on the wall or in the floor. If you do, you'll be impaled. Watching out for Gargoyles, go down three flights and head right. At the end of the ledge, go down—but stop before you reach the second pillar. The floor beside it is false and will drop you to your death. Leap it, continue right, ascend one flight, and go right a bit more. See that glowing orb? Shoot it with the Oak Stake, and you'll be rewarded with Dracula's rib. Go left, only this time fall through the fake floor at the pillar to get to the bottom. Go left to leave. Now . . . you can trace your way back to the beginning of the game, or you can take the easy way out: let yourself die. You can get back to the start, fully armed with all the weapons you've earned, by inputting the following code: ZOJJ BGRY UI2X XWI3. Note: the "O" is the letter O, not a zero, and the two "I's" are the letter I, not ones.

Starting from the top-left level of the first village again, go down a flight, then jump off the ledge to the left and go left. Continue left, through the Forest, whipping Zombie Hands and other monsters, earning 200 Hearts so you'll be able to purchase the Morning Star. Wade through the lava to the left and stop at the Ferryman; he'll take you across the lake. When you reach the shore, continue left, passing through the town to the Forest (where you'll battle some fire-breathing Dragons and more Blobs). When you reach the steps, go down one flight only and jump off the ledge to the left (make sure you take a hefty jump, so you'll miss the false blocks in the floor). Go left, and step down carefully from this ledge, onto the first block on the next ledge. (*Don't* jump onto the ledge: blocks two and three are an illusion!) Leap over the false floor to the next ledge on the left. Enter the Graveyard and go left. When you reach the dead end, throw Garlic and a shrouded figure will appear to give you a Silk Bag. This will enable you to carry a larger stock of healing potions. (By the way, whenever you heave Garlic, none of your throwing weapons—knives, Holy Water, etc. —will work . . . just the Whip. These weapons won't be restored to you until you've passed from the screen with the Garlic. Also when using Garlic, make sure you pitch it to the ground, not into the water. It'll only work on land.)

Return the way you came, to the right (it's okay to wade through the lava you'll encounter, since you can't use the ledges from this approach). Climb the steps, and when you've climbed to the top of all the flights, go left. When you reach the town, stay on the bottom, traipse all the way to the left side, go up the steps, turn right, and enter the first open door. Inside, descend until you meet the shrouded figure who will sell you the Morning Star—the longest and most powerful whip of all. From here, go back to where you started the game; or else take the short cut by resetting the game and punching in the following code: EHQC CJEY ZN1E—that's "one," not "i"—S7JG.

Advanced Strategy: The next item on your agenda should be obtaining the Silver Knife, which is more powerful than the Dagger. Go right, on the bottom, through the village. You'll pass, in turn, the Forest, the River, more Forest, the Mansion, still more Forest (stay on the top level), the Dungeon where you got the Flame (stay on the top level), yet another Forest, a town, and the Graveyard. Throw some Garlic, and the shrouded figure will appear to give you the Knife. Return to the village where you started (or hit reset, and use the code DYG2 LGT0 ("zero," not "O") UO8H ("O," not "zero") T5RX.

At the upper left of the first village once more, you start by going down one flight, jumping to the bottom, and heading right through the Forest, River, Dungeon (on the top level), and another Forest. When you reach the Mansion, enter. Use the Crystal to see the invisible elevator as before, then kill the Knight on the right and proceed that way. Continue right through the Forest (top level), Dungeon (top level), next Forest (note where the staircase is), and village. Stay on the bottom of the village, and when you reach the town limits on the right, ascend two flights and go left. When you meet the Knight, have a chat with him; he'll offer to exchange his Crystal for the one you have. Do so. And make sure you do so on the first try; if you back away or ask a second time, he won't want to bargain with you.

To get to this point automatically, you can use the code TIDK (that's "I," not "one") L8TZ WO8F ("O," not "zero") 50J1 ("zero," not "O," and "one," not "I"). Return to the staircase you were told to note (above), and enter the cave. Climb the ledges and go to the River. Kneel at the bank by pressing down with the joystick; after 5 seconds stairs will appear at the edge of the water. Descend and go right, to the Mansion. Be on your guard here, for the Freddies don't just attack, they throw deadly bones at you. Continue right on the bottom. When you reach the first stone wall, walk right through it; it's a fake. Buy an Oak Stake from the shrouded figure amid the spiked pits, then go left to the stairs and up three flights. Head right and up the first set of stairs. Jump up the L-shaped ledges to the next set of stairs, climb, then jump up more L-shaped blocks. Go right when you reach the level just below the ceiling. Descend the first set of stairs, head left, and go down to the bottom. Head right; when you see the Orb, destroy it with the Stake to obtain Dracula's Heart. Return to where you began this level in the village, or hit reset and use the code DYEM LFD0 ("zero," not "O") UO8H ("O," not "zero") TZJX.

Again, starting out: go down a flight of steps, leap to the bottom, and walk left. Traverse the Forest, take a big jump and wade through the lava (you'll lose some energy, but this will be replenished), and stop at the Ferryman. Show him Dracula's Heart and he'll take you to where you need to go. When you reach land, get off and go left to the Mansion. Enter, go right and up the stairs for three flights. Turn left, go up two flights of stairs, head right, climb two flights of stairs and go right again. In the new screen climb down the ledges, go right (the Gargoyles here surrender special Hearts when slain), climb down the steps (be prepared to slay the Knight waiting for you at the bottom), and go right. Step into the niche in the floor and claim the Book for an important clue. Leave the niche and go left—though not back up the steps. You'll see a shrouded figure as you continue to the left; buy an Oak Stake, 'cause you'll be needing it real soon.

Go down the ledges to the steps, descend three flights and go right, into the tunnel; in the next room to the right you'll battle the large, flying, scythe-tossing Grim Reaper. However, the monster's blades are fairly easy to dodge, and a series of blows from your Whip will destroy the big, purple bully. When it perishes, you'll acquire the potent Gold Knife. Go right, into the next chamber; poke the Orb there with a Stake, and Dracula's yummy Eyeball will be all yours!

Leave and return to the outside of the Mansion, go left to the River and cross the Floating Blocks. (These are easy to cross . . . though you'll need a running jump to land on the first, and small running jumps to hit most of the successive blocks. To do this, stand as far to the right of each block as you can without falling off. This will give you the oomph you need to make the leaps.) When you reach the left bank, go to the shrouded figure and get the Diamond. This is a nifty weapon: you can fire huge Diamonds in rapid succession (that is, you don't have to wait until one is off the screen before you fire the next).

Here's the code that will get you this far in the game: 7QJ4 O5FV ("O," not "zero") 154J ("one," not "I") XXR5. If you want to go even farther along without having to break a sweat (coward!), the code to use is FPIV ("I," not "one") MUSC 1ZSY ("one," not "I") VGZO ("O," not "zero"). The skills and weapons you've acquired to date are pretty much all you'll need, until you face the king of the vampires himself. When he appears, you can hit him for a few seconds before he moves. Use this time to get in your licks (with the Flame Whip), then stay on the left side. Drac'll start flying around, throwing batlike Frisbees; use your Laurels to defend yourself, while you lash at his putrid self. The ol' fang-ster isn't that tough to beat.

Par: A good player should be able to get as far as the Heart. After that, the monsters come at you faster and more furiously, especially inside the Mansion.

Training Tips: Skip the powerful Whips, and use Holy Water only to break down barriers, and see how far you get. If you learn how to protect yourself with the least useful Whip, you'll do super-well when you obtain the more powerful models! It's also a good idea to use the codes to go to advanced levels and use low-power weapons to battle monsters during the night. If that challenge doesn't "whip" you into shape, nothing will!

Rating: As you can see, this is a complex cartridge with a lot to discover and map. Only one complaint: unlike the first game, all of the landscape here is more or less the same. Forest, village, River, Mansion . . . boredom! Some variety would have been nice. But then, with all the monsters swarming around, most players won't have time to do much sightseeing.

Challenge: B+
Graphics: B
Sound Effects: A (dynamite music!)

CHAPTER TEN

COBRA COMMAND

Type: Helicopter shoot-'em-up.

Manufacturer: Data East, under license from Nintendo.

Objective: Hostages are being held in various South Pacific and Indonesian lands. Your mission: to fly your Cobra chopper in and rescue them.

Layout: The screen scrolls horizontally through six levels, with a handful of vertical drops and ascents.

Hero: Your Cobra attack chopper is extremely maneuverable, and can aim its missiles at various angles. It also picks up more powerful armaments as it travels through enemy territory; information on these can be found in the two *Strategy* sections.

Enemies: There are various helicopters, artillery, and missiles, which are discussed below.

Menu: There's only the one-player game.

Scoring: You earn points for the number of enemies destroyed and hostages rescued.

Beginner's Strategy: Here's a mission-by-mission breakdown of the rescue operation.

Sumatra: There are twenty hostages being held here. After collecting the first two hostages (easy), blast the round top of the first structure you see. Continue firing until the building falls apart (it'll shake the first time you hit it, which tells you you're on target). An underground tunnel awaits: fly in. Shoot the green Block, continue onward, land on the roof to get the Turbo Engine and Guns there. As you advance along the next underground passage, move toward the left wall slowly. There will be less wall in view, and, thus, fewer Tanks shooting at you from underneath. There are three hostages in the last structure at the end of the passageway. Destroy the Tank, save three more hostages, fight another tank, and rescue one more hostage. Before flying from the passage, wait over the building on the second level. The Missile Truck will leave without firing at you. Get out of the passage, and rescue a hostage on the first tower on the right. Next up: getting past the Missile Silos. Pass between the first two, edge ahead, put on the brakes, and repeat until you're through. When you come to a building with a star, blast the star. The structure will collapse, revealing another underground passage. When you come to a Silo with a circle, shoot it or you won't be able to continue. Head right, land on the flat roof to get the Twin Missiles, and blast the Missile Car which will show up moments later. Collect three more hostages, fight another Car, save three more men, fight a third Car, save another three soldiers, destroy a fourth Car, rescue one hostage and leave . . . keeping an eye out for the soldiers who will be waiting for you as you depart!

Java: There are 28 hostages to be saved. Save a hostage on the green platform, then blast the circle on top of the building to open the underground passage. Fly down and shoot the blue circles so you can continue. Land on the first blue roof to pick up the Super Engine and Fire Bomb. Alight between the two blue buildings so you can destroy the Missile Tank, save three hostages, battle the next Missile Tank, save three more men, fight the Tank, save another three men, bash the Tank, collect three more men, do in the Tank, save one hostage, then fly ahead. A blue tower will rise up from the earth; get around it, then save a hostage from the top of the brown tower just beyond it. When you spot the brown circle on the top of the building, blast it and enter the tunnel. Shoot the gryphon's head to get into the left passage behind it, and enter. Land on the flat blue roof to pick up Armor and Homing Missiles, shoot the blue circle on the right, and keep going through the passage. Rescue three hostages and fight the Missile Tank (repeat this three times), save one hostage—and you're home free!

Borneo: You've got to save 27 hostages here. The key to surviving this level is to fly backward. Most of your enemies will be coming at you from that direction! Go to the right side of the shack to save a hostage, return to the left side of the building located before it to rescue another man, shoot the overhang of the building on the left to access the underground passage. Shell the left/top brown structure to continue. Go to the bottom left and settle down on the flat brown roof: pick up the Hyper Engine, Mines, and Ladder. Shoot the Crate, destroy the Missile Tank, and continue down the tunnel . . . to the oft-repeated refrain: save three hostages and battle the Missile Tank. Do this three more times (a total of four times), then return to the beginning of the underground passage and skedaddle. After passing the fire and water, blast the tower on the left side of the building there, to go into another tunnel. Blast the big green building on the right (making sure you dodge the Columns, which have a tendency to come crashing down at the most inopportune times). Shoot the brown circle to continue, and enter the green-brown doors to procure the Homing Missiles and Anti-Tank Guns. Then: pick up three hostages, fight the Tank, and repeat three times. Save the last, lone hostage, and it's on to the fourth mission!

Advanced Strategy:

South China Sea: There are 29 hostages on this level. Blast the blue section at the front of the boat and fly in. There are three hostages on the right. Blast the Missile Carrier, save three more men, battle the Missile Carrier, ditto again, then save the one remaining soldier. Leave the boat, shooting to the right. Keep firing away, and when you see the first tower on the island, blast the left side of the blue door. Pass underground, land on the roof of the red building and collect more Homing Missiles. Fly backward, near the ground, and go left. Pick up the three hostages, then fly right, still going backward. Leave the tunnel . . . being prepared to duck as the Super-Destroyer launches a Homing Missile of its own! Destroy the topmost Radar Base on the Volcano and enter the underground passage. Blast the red building and continue, then fire away at the twin red circles in order to keep going. Fly to the oddly-shaped building (the one that looks like a refugee from a seafood restaurant), and stop just above the red ledge on the right wall on the left-facing room. Turn the Homing Missiles loose on the Tank. Save three men, battle the Missile Carrier—and repeat four more times. Save the one remaining hostage, and head to—

Siam: Just seven guys to save here; you've got it easy. (Sure. If you fly backward most of the time and collect the special weapons, you have a chance.) Fly until you come to the building with the green circle on top. Shoot it and enter the underground passage. Make your way to the second platform, collect the weapons, move to the third platform, save the three hostages, battle the Super Tank, repeat, save the one hostage, blast the lion head, and you're through.

Enemy Headquarters: No hostages here . . . just the bad guys. Pass the first Fire Ball, slow down, and hover when the edge of the next Fire Ball appears. Fly backward, to the right. Shoot the bottom head on the building, and fly into the tunnel. Go slowly through the Fire Balls, and shoot the brown circle atop the Columns. Fly backward into the tunnel. Edge forward, past the Fire Balls, and destroy the head on the building. End of enemy . . . and your mission.

Par: Scores vary too widely to come up with a meaningful average. Some players go slowly so they can blast as many enemy craft and installations as possible; other players are concerned only about the hostages and keep destruction to a minimum. We will say this, however: a good player will be able to rescue all of the hostages on the first four missions.

Training Tips: The most vital skill is being able to shift the angle of your Cobra ship so you can aim its guns quickly. Practice handling the craft in the *Sumatra* mission until you've got this ability down pat.

Rating: An action-filled war game; the versatile helicopter is a welcome change of pace from

all the tanks and shirtless, Rambo-style mercenaries in the other war games.
Challenge: B
Graphics: B—
Sound Effects: B

CHAPTER ELEVEN

DEFENDER OF THE CROWN

Type: Varieties of medieval combat—sort of a *Track and Field* for knights.

Manufacturer: Ultra Software, under license from Nintendo.

Objective: The place: England. The time: 1149 A.D. Six lords are battling for the throne, three of them Saxons, three Normans. Initially, the Saxons are your allies, but as time passes you'll be more and more on your own. Your goal is to claim all the Castles on the map.

Layout: There are many different kinds of screens: a map, side views of battle, overhead views of combat, and the warrior's point of view of an attacker.

Hero: You can choose one of four lords, each of whom has different powers as described in the instruction booklet. The weapons you will be called upon to use are Lance, Morning Star

87

(mace), Sword, Catapult (you are permitted to hurl Greek Fire, Disease, or Boulders against the enemy), and Crossbow. Unfortunately, your fate is not always in your hands (see *Enemies*).

Enemies: Each encounter you make is a Turn. Time passes between each Turn; in the interim, the computer may cause battles to be waged on the map of England, which redistribute the power . . . your own included. The stronger you are, the better your chances of successfully defending a besieged Castle. However, the more land you conquer, the more often the computer sends rival lords on Raids to steal your gold. There is no protection against these forays.

Menu: There is only the one-player game.

Scoring: The player earns Income from combat victories, and uses it to buy Soldiers and Knights. These are automatically dumped onto your Home Castle, and it's up to you to distribute them throughout your holdings as you see fit. However, you can place no more than 250 soldiers in any one Castle (and no less than 20, though it's suicidal to have less than 100). You can also buy the services of Robin Hood (up to three times), a valuable asset when you make your own Raids.

Beginner's Strategy: We're going to make this game really simple for you. When you choose which Knight you're going to be, select Wolfric the Wild. He's great at jousting, and though he's weak at leadership and sword-play, that won't matter. Winning the joust, he'll face a weakened opponent in the mace battle that follows, thus winning the entire contest. And there's nothing like winning a joust to bring you fame and boost your leader-ship qualities. As for being weak in swordplay at the start: no sweat. Hire Robin Hood for the first few raids, build up your bank account, hire armies, and who cares about your ability to swing a blade? What's more, the computer randomly has your knight challenged to jousts by other knights. Anyone but Wolfric can suffer serious setbacks in these, not just by losing, but by jousting badly—hitting your opponent's horse, for example. Such un-becoming conduct can cost you all your prop-erty! (Your best bet, no matter which knight you are, is to aim for the shield.) About the only benefit to picking Geoffrey Longsword, who is Mr. Swordsmanship himself, is that he's sure to triumph when called upon to res-cue a captured princess. That will win him the woman's father as an ally . . . but only temporarily. In the end it's still every knight for himself. And better to be Wolfric under those circumstances.

As for battles between armies, requiring the Catapults and Crossbow, there are really very few strategies. Check page 11 of your instruc-tion booklet to see which tactic will best serve your particular situation. However, "Hold Your Ground" is the most dependable. Thus, wait until your situation is such that it fits the requirements for "Hold Your Ground" before starting a battle. Above all, patience, rather than recklessness, is the way to win this game; don't spread your armies thin!

Advanced Strategy: Fine-tuning your battle skills is something you can use to help swing events in your favor. For example, when you wheel out the old Catapult, strike the Castle wall with two or three Boulders; hit it right where the tower and wall meet, to the left of the tower. After you've made a good-sized hole, hurl in Disease and (if you've any shots left) fling some Greek Fire for good measure. As for the Crossbow, this is easy. Your adversaries usually appear left, right, left, right, forcing you to shift from side to side (costing you time and forcing you to re-aim). Start moving in another direction as soon as your opponent goes tumbling over the wall.

Par: Playing even a fairly cautious game, keeping all your castles stocked with soldiers, you should be able to win this one in approximately three hours.

Training Tips: Having said that you should play the game with caution, it's also a good exercise to try it in a bare-bones mode: attack when you're least prepared. That'll give you a chance to see the worst-possible-case scenarios the game has to offer.

Rating: Give the Ultra people credit for trying to do a videogame version of classic board games like *Risk* and *Castle Risk*. The problem here is that while looking at the map and distributing your armies is a diverting strategic challenge, the battles themselves are much too pedestrian.

Challenge: C—

Graphics: B+ (Very good animation, with some startling artwork during transitions from the joust, meeting Robin Hood, etc.)

Sound Effects: C— (A few okay sound effects, but the music should have been more stirring and/or medieval.)

CHAPTER TWELVE

FIST OF THE NORTH STAR

Type: Martial arts bash-'em-up.

Manufacturer: Taxan, under license from Nintendo.

Objective: Ken's people are being oppressed by a nasty bunch of bosses. Sick and tired of his peoples' misery, Ken ventures forth to destroy the tyrants and their minions.

Layout: The screen scrolls horizontally, with a rare staircase that leads diagonally. There are eight different levels.

Hero: Ken is a tall, lean fighting machine who can jump, walk, crouch, and both punch and kick while doing any of the above movements. He acquires Stars from many beaten foes, which boost his strength. He can earn a Gold Necklace which stops the timer for 5 seconds, makes Ken invulnerable for that period, and also splits him into two Kens so he can double his conquests. He can also find a Silver Necklace, which gives him Shooting Power (the ability to fire flurries of punches or kicks). This power is also acquired after he's beaten 20 foes. (If you have the NES Advantage, this power won't benefit you: it's the same as playing the game with Turbo.)

Enemies: There are eight bosses: Bask, Gayler, Tiger, Solia, Blue Light Bolts, Red Light Bolts, Gold Falco, and Shula, and they have powers that are described in the *Strategy* sections. There are also ninja-like guards and soldiers working for each boss, as well as sub-bosses who are more powerful than the mere warriors and fight you alone.

Menu: There's only the one-player game.

Scoring: In addition to the power-up items, you earn points for killing foes. These begin at the 300- and 400-point level for each flunky in the early stages, and go up to thousands of points for the bosses (see booklet for a breakdown of the latter). Point values rise as Ken makes his way deeper into the realm. Stars reward you with several thousand points apiece. Ken races against a timer, which varies from screen to screen.

Beginner's Strategy: One point that is valid for all levels: don't ever let the bosses pin you in a corner. With the exception of the surprisingly weak Bask, they'll beat or blast the heck out of you!

The level-by-level guide is as follows:

Bask: Head right through his "Country Capital," punching and kicking your way through the easy foes here; one of the early enemies usually gives you a Gold Necklace. The first sub-boss appears at roughly the 75-second mark and is easy to beat. Gameplay is pretty much the same as you fight your way to Bask. As soon as he arrives, get in close and throw your punches, then back away to avoid his violent response. Immediately get in close to him again and repeat. He'll go down quickly.

Gayler: The so-called "City Group" is a little tougher than the lot run by Bask: they throw things at you, and their labyrinthine headquarters are mazelike. Go to the right, on the bottom level. Jump to the top level at the first break. Climb the steps, go right on the upper level, climb the steps, and go left. Hop up to the ramp, climb the steps, go right, and fight the sub-boss using crouch and kick together and getting in close, hitting him repeatedly. He'll go down in a sec. Head right to the first pit (just beyond the red door), and descend. Go down a series of pits, go right, then head upstairs. Go right and fight the Sumo-type boss, who's going to be throwing things at you. Get in and kick him, ducking when he starts flinging weapons, or leap over him when he tries to muscle you into a corner. Repeat until he's defeated.

Tiger: He runs the "Traitor Concentration Camp," where the guards toss knives and clubs. Go right, into the door (where you'll usually get the Gold Necklace). The sub-boss arrives quickly (at approximately the 80-second mark) and jumps and cracks a whip. Leap when he does, kicking him in midair, and also kick him on the ground using a hit-and-back-away technique, so his whip won't get you. When you finish with him, go right, kicking down the walls so you can proceed. When ol' Tiger comes at you with his Green Light Fireballs, get in close and hit him, leap back when he fires, jumping the Fireballs, then come in and resume your attack. He's not too tough.

Solia: His "Army" consists of more blade-tossing flunkies who tend to show up in pairs. You'll usually get a Gold Necklace early in the struggle, which makes things easy. Solia is a virtual rehash of Tiger, with his Purple Light Fireballs. Fight him the same way, though it'll take a little more effort to bring him down.

Advanced Strategy: Continuing your crusade:

Blue Light Bolts: This is a short stage, in which you fight punks who seem to have been cloned from the last level. If you got this far, there's nothing special you need to know.

Red Light Bolts: His "Army" is pretty strong, and the challenge is greater here because whatever bricks you're standing on often crumble, allowing Ken to plunge to his death. Fortunately, there's a solution. In addition to the floor, there are platforms midway up the screen and at top; stick to these as much as possible, so if you fall, at least you'll land on the floor or the platform beneath, and not in a bottomless pit somewhere below your TV set. If upper platforms are blocked by the red walls, never fear: you can go up and punch 'em down. At the beginning, head right, climb the steps, get off on the first floor, stay on the upper platforms, and get set for the big sub-boss, who arrives at approximately the 35-second mark. Though he looks imposing, you can defeat him easily using a crouch-kick combo. Since all of the soldiers on this level will be throwing things at you, be prepared to duck . . : but also beware the guys who come sliding in at you at superspeed. When you crouch, keep kicking toward the right, so you can derail one of these speedsters as he rushes in and tries to hurt you. You'll meet twins of the sub-boss several times on this level before you reach the end. Fight the main boss here as you did the earlier Light throwers. (Note: we have no idea why the game calls the boss Jakko and the instructions call him Red Light Bolts. It's one of those unanswerable mysteries of life.)

Gold Falco: His level, and his powers, are similar to what's gone before. Again, if you've gotten to the seventh level, you won't need our help.

Shula: For the last boss, he's pretty easy to take out . . . though at least he's different from the bosses who came before. He has a kick that'll knock you into another cartridge if it connects. Don't let it! Keep jumping, and get in your own blows when you can. The two of you will look like Mexican Jumping Beans as you bound around the screen, but if you keep your distance and slip in for blows when you see an opening, you'll have no trouble.

Par: If you make your way through each level slowly, killing as many enemies as you want (there's an unlimited supply!), you're going to earn more points than someone who hurries through. Still, most players average 30,000 points for the first two levels; 40,000 points for the third and fourth; and 60,000 points thereafter.

Training Tips: There's a practice mode; using it, you'll be able to run through all the skills you'll be needing.

Rating: The game is great for novice players; veterans will find little to challenge them here. It also doesn't help that most of the foes and screens are so similar.
  Challenge: C
  Graphics: B+
  Sound Effects: B−

CHAPTER THIRTEEN

FRIDAY THE 13TH

Type: Horror quest.

Manufacturer: LJN, under license from Nintendo.

Objective: You're a camp Counselor who's about to be put on permanent summer vacation. The mad monster Jason is stalking you, and you've got to search the grounds of Crystal Lake to find the various weapons that will stop him. Problem is, several other gruesome natives are after your blood, so you must proceed with diligence and caution.

Layout: The screen scrolls from side to side as you make your way around the campgrounds. Outside the cabins, the view is from the Counselor's side; inside the cabin, you're looking out over the Counselor's shoulder. The Map screen is an overhead view of the area, and a cabin lights up whenever someone is in danger (meaning that you should race there, pronto).

Hero: You can take the part of one of six counselors, each of whom has certain abilities. When it comes to running, jumping, and fighting, Crissy and Mark are the stars. The other four Counselors are merely adequate in all areas. The weapons you can obtain are listed in the instruction booklet and are also discussed below.

Enemies: Jason is one powerful nutcase, though his mother (her head guards his weapons) isn't chopped liver either. The problem with these two Voorhees is that when they're slain, they don't stay dead; worse, they return stronger than before. The other monsters—Zombies (both land and water breeds), Wolves, Crows, and Bats—though plentiful, are easy to slay, compared to the Voorhees.

Menu: There's only the one-player game.

Scoring: The game begins with 15 children in jeopardy; the scoreboard ticks them off as you rescue them. One of two 60-second clocks begins running whenever Jason has cornered a Child (bottom clock) or a Counselor (top clock). You also play for weapons, trying to obtain more powerful ones as you make your way through the campground.

Beginner's Strategy: To answer the question most commonly asked about this game: no. There are no patterns to Jason's comings-and-goings, or to the appearances of the weapons. Luck and chance are the name of the game.

About the only thing you can count on is that there'll be more monsters afoot at sunset.

When it comes to dealing with the lesser monsters, the Zombies are easy to kill (four stones or three dagger shots will destroy one), while the Wolves are best dealt with by ducking when they appear, spinning to face them, and firing. When it comes time to face Jason, if you meet him on a path, go to the opposite side from which he entered, wait until he comes to that side, leap over him, run to the opposite side, and start shooting. The fact that you lured him to the other side before leaping him gives you more time to fire at him before he reaches you. Even if you can't make it all the way to the other side, make sure you jump over him. If you just stand there and face his attack, you're going to go straight from the camp to the morgue. If you meet Jason in a cabin, position yourself so that you're slightly to the right of the N in the word JASON over his energy meter. Why there? Because you can lean and avoid Jason's blows when he attacks, yet you're so close to the left wall that you effectively prevent Jason from coming at you on that side. He'll mill about only in front of you and on the right, which will also make it easier for you to draw a bead on him and fire.

Perhaps the key strategy when you're not in a fight situation is to use the Lighter (which will appear early in the game) to light the Fireplaces in the six biggest Cabins. When all are roaring, you'll get the Flashlight. Use this to help you find Jason's mother when you go to the Cave. (Why would you want to do something dangerous like visit the Cave? Because when you destroy Mrs. Voorhees, your weapon is one-upped, making you more powerful.) Lighting all the Fireplaces will also cause the Axe, Machete, and Torch to become available to you in the cabins.

Advanced Strategy: As you become more experienced and learn your way around the campgrounds, you'll become better at protecting your key assets: Crissy and Mark. These are your strongest Counselors, so you'll want to preserve them from damage as much as possible. Use other Counselors for the early work, and pass powerful weapons to your two stars as you obtain them. However, don't bring them into play until absolutely necessary. And, of course, race to their rescue as fast as you can if they're ever cornered by Jason.

The "passing of weapons" aspect of *Friday the 13th* is the key to keeping the game going. As you obtain Daggers in the early phase of the play, pass them to other Counselors so they'll be armed. That way, when you're taking the part of another Counselor, those you've left behind will suffer less harm when Jason corners and attacks them.

Par: You should be able to rescue an average of ten kids before Jason really starts to get on your nerves (and back and face).

Training Tips: The smartest thing any player can do is to make a map of the inside of each cabin. Otherwise, you can waste a lot of time trying to find your way to the Fireplaces or back to the door. Also map the Cave, since that will not only make Mrs. Voorhees easier to find, but it'll remind you where the pits and high ledges are. If you're in a hurry while you're there, you'll want to know what's ahead . . . right?

Rating: Most players agree: the videogame is not as good as it should or could have been if players had taken the part of Jason, not the Counselors. Parents and store owners probably would've objected to kids pretending to be a killer (they did with the old Atari-compatible game *The Texas Chainsaw Massacre),* but that's baloney; it's sort of like claiming that a perfectly normal actor shouldn't star in *Macbeth* for fear he'll run out and kill someone. As a result, we've got a game that's simply a notch above average.

Challenge: C+

Graphics: B (The character animation is *feh,* but the scenery and the way it moves as you do is very well done.)

Sound Effects: C (There's none of the famous "breathing" music, and why doesn't anyone *scream* in this game?)

CHAPTER FOURTEEN

THE GUARDIAN LEGEND

Type: Science fiction shoot-'em-up.

Manufacturer: Broderbund, under license from Nintendo.

Objective: Eons ago, aliens sent a world called Naju toward earth. Naju was laden with various life forms which turned evil during the long journey. Now, as Naju nears earth, you must penetrate its labyrinthine exterior and interior to find Keys and activate the ten self-destruct mechanisms that will destroy the world and its monstrous cargo.

Layout: The screen scrolls in all directions; the view is from overhead. There's also a map screen that tells you where you are and where you need to go.

Hero: While you're exploring the surface, you exist in human form. When you first fly to the world, and later venture into its bowels, you take the form of an airborne fighter. In either shape, you pack a basic weapon with unlimited firepower. As you murder monsters, many will turn over an Optional Weapon or important Item—such as a Shield, Energy Tanks, Pyramids (secret passages), and so on. There are 25 varieties of Weapon or Item; these are discussed in the instructions and below. You lose energy whenever aliens shoot or touch you; if your life gauge reaches zero, you've had it.

Enemies: The major creatures are listed in the instructions. All appear only at the end of the underground/undersea levels, and must be defeated before the prize, there, can be claimed. Several of these monsters are discussed in detail below. There are also many creatures on the surface of the world. Most of these are spidery things that are easily destroyed; the exceptions are the monsters who appear when the siren sounds. When you hear this, you can either stand and fight, or run; if you wait too long, you'll have no choice but to fight, since blocks form around you to box you and the monster in.

Menu: There's only the one-player game.

Scoring: You earn points by killing monsters and shooting Yellow Pyramids. More importantly, you roam the planet collecting Chips. The number of these you have determines how often you can fire your Optional Weapon.

Beginner's Strategy: On your approach to the planet, don't just play the bottom of the screen. Scoot to the center, climbing over the projectiles you've missed, so that you're not overwhelmed by those plus the new projectiles pouring in from the top. When the doors begin opening on the sides and disgorging missiles, adopt a figure-eight pattern to blast the doors as they open, and avoid the projectiles. At the end of this run you'll come to a mass of doors like the ones you just fought. When you first arrive, take out one row of three vertical doors on the left or right with a steady stream of fire. Then pick off the single doors on the end and return to deal with the last two rows of three.

When you land on Naju's surface, notice that every screen has coordinates. Note these as you travel. (We've provided several in our discussion below, as landmarks.) Also, you'll be confronted by three kinds of Pyramids: the aforementioned Yellow, which only give you points (and often form Arrows or Letters on the ground); Red, which are indestructible; and Green, which, when shot, become Blue and give you access to special rooms. Please be aware that what's described below is just *one* way to travel; a way that will give you all twelve Option Weapons and two Keys. Obviously, you can blaze your own trail through Naju. You can also pause to blast Yellow Pyramids and fight the aliens that quickly cluster around them. Try to get all the Pyramids, but also be reasonable; if there are too many monsters, don't be ashamed to split!

To begin, walk to the left as far as you can,

then up to get Red Lander, which boosts the maximum number of Chips you can collect. Avoid the left passage and go up (to X8Y9), blasting the Green Pyramid to acquire MultiBullets. Go back to the right, continuing all the way to X14Y9. When you hear the Siren, stay put: battle the monster and get the Blue Lander it leaves behind. Go down to the dead end on the left, keep left, and shoot the Pyramids at X9Y14. You'll be rewarded with a Saber Laser. Keep left until you reach the dead end, then go up. At X8Y13 stop at the Siren, fight the extraterrestrial, and claim the Bullet Shield. Go up to X8Y10, then left to X7Y10. Enter X6Y10, enter the hole left by shooting the Blue Pyramid. Shoot the other Blue Pyramid in the room, and the Platform in the center will open. Leap in, and you'll become the ship.

This is an underwater battle scene, in which you fight fish and plants of all kinds. The most interesting life form you'll encounter (it's okay to do some sightseeing and be in awe!) is a black ball that unzips the ground. When you meet it, follow it and shoot the heck out of the sucker. Otherwise, it'll release monsters. Nothing will give you much trouble until you reach the end (you're almost there when you claim the Power Heart). A Fleepa will appear, releasing deadly fish at you. Slide from side to side; whenever the giant rises, pause beneath it and shoot up. When you're victorious, you'll earn your first Key. When you automatically return to room X6Y10, claim the Optional Weapon (Repeller) there. Exit using the hole at top. Go up, left, then down at the dead end. Shoot the square of Pyramids at X3Y10 and get the Back Fire Optional Weapon here. This isn't a powerful weapon, but it's great if you're surrounded. Head left, then enter the hole at the top of the room guarded by the turniplike monster. If you wish to stop here (or jump right to this point), the code to use is: uiIg PuZf Mikc Iekd DXMc DOYy QOT3 GtS3.

Head left, then up to the dead end, left, up at the dead end (blasting the square of Pyramids for Chips), and into the hole at the top (X1Y8). Open the Platform as before, and you'll find yourself underwater once more. Everything is pretty much the same as before, only this time you'll be fighting Optomon at the end. This cyclopean beast descends from the top, unleashing strings of Seaweed and balls of Algae at the bottom of the screen. Go to the dead center of the screen and blast away; do just a bit of jiggling left and right as necessary. When you beat the monster and return to X1Y8, you'll be rewarded with a Grenade.

Leave the room, go down, right, down, and left at the Pyramid Arrow. Go down, right at the next Arrow, down at the Arrow, then right where the next Arrow points left. Continue right to the square or Pyramids; blast them to obtain the Cutter Laser. Go up and fight the monster crab at the Siren—its claws spit deadly bubbles; shoot its soft underbelly when the monster spreads these claws. When it dies, you'll get the Fireball Option. Go left and up, then right to X4Y8. Continue until you reach X1Y8, enter the hole on the top, then travel left and up to fight the monster at the dead end. Circle the room clockwise, shooting the creature in the center of the room. Get the Red Lander when it dies. Go down, right, and make sure you shoot the spider alien here before it has a chance to reproduce. It'll split, and then each creature it's spawned will also split. Needless to say, that adds up to a lot of monsters if you don't vaporize it at once.

Enter the hole and return to X1Y8. (Why didn't you just stay there? You needed Chips, so make sure you reap 'em!) Leave, go down, right, down, right (to X3Y10), up, right at the dead end, down at the next dead end (X6Y9), and enter the hole at the bottom. You're now in X6Y10. Go right, up, right, down, and into the hole at X9Y10. In X9Y11 enter the bottom hole. Go right, into the right hole at X10Y12. Enter the right hole and emerge in X12Y12. Get Consecutive Firing from the Pyramids there. Go right, to X14Y12, down, left, up at the S-shaped Pyramids, and into X11Y12. Enter the hole at the top, go up, then turn right at X11Y9. When you reach X14Y9, head down. Take a left at the dead end. When you reach the next dead end, head left and enter the hole to room X6Y13. Leave and go down, head left, up, and left to X4Y14. Enter the hole and open the Platform: sail up and battle the Fleepa here as before. Your reward will be a Hyper Laser. When you emerge in X4Y15, leave at the bottom and continue down. At the left-pointing Arrow, go right. Fight the monster crab here as before and obtain the Gun Item. Go left, over the Arrow, following it this time. Follow the red markers until you reach X0Y15. Go up, right, and fight the monster here as you did before—only this time, using a counterclockwise motion. You'll need the Red Lander it provides. When you're victorious, go right, get the Blue Lander at X3Y14, head down, left, and into the hole at X2Y15. Walk on or shoot all four corner Platforms to open the one in the center. At the end of this battle site you'll face a Crawdaddy, whose deadly claws reach far and wave quickly from side to side, releasing lethal fish. Use the Bullet Shield Option and Gun Item here. When you're victorious, you'll get a Key and, back in the room, a second Saber Laser (don't avoid getting "doubles" of Options: they make the first one more powerful). Leave the room at the top. Go left, down (following the red path), right, up at the Arrow, right, down, right, and up to X6Y14. Enter the room for your code, which is: qUbD LAXC kVcC GcsA HRUG ?z?j IbZ5 UEU8

Advanced Strategy: Leave the room. In X7Y13 go right, up, right at the dead end, down to X9Y10, into the hole at the bottom, out the next hole to X9Y12, left, down to X8Y14, and into the hole at the bottom. You're now in X8Y16. Go down, left, down (over the two Arrows), left at the dead end, and leave *fast,* heading up, so you won't have to battle the monster just yet. (If you choose to fight, use Fireball.) Shoot the Pyramid square to get the Red Lander, then go left, up, left, up, left, down, left, up, left, and fight the monster in X1Y20. You'll win the Enemy Eraser here. Go left, down to X0Y23, get a clue by entering the Blue Pyramid, go right to the end, then go down and fight the monster you avoided before, armed with your Enemy Eraser. When you kill it, go up and left at X7Y20 and into the hole at the left. Enter Corridor 13. Instead of a sea world this time, you'll be soaring through a prehistoric jungle. At the end you'll face Bombarder, who materializes, fires a slew of you-seeking Missiles, then dematerializes. Use the Bullet Shield for protection, and dash under Bombarder, firing up into its center whenever it appears. It'll take a billion or so hits to destroy it, but be patient. You'll be rewarded with a Shield, which boosts your defensive power.

You're back in Corridor 13 now. To the left is the hole leading to Corridor 3; go there if you want, though you'd be wiser to wait until you're more completely armed. So, leave by the right, go up, right, up, into the hole and out (you're in X8Y14), up, right, enter the right hole, then go into the next right hole. Enter the hole at the top, go to the top again, then head right. In X13Y11 you'll be able to buy some Option Weapons using Chips. Do so: purchase the Area Blaster, a second Back

Fire, and a Wave Attack. You now have all the Options.

Leave and go left, down, into the left hole, into another left hole, down at the W shape formed by the Pyramids, then down into the hole at the dead end. You can now return to Corridor 13 and enter Corridor 3, to face the more powerful Optomon here. The code, just prior to going back to Corridor 13, is: z6ig Uiyg t7Yf NG1f (letter l) S?Nw qSY5 BnPm y8qa

Par: Since players can move in any direction they want, in any order they wish, there's no average score.

Training Tips: Use one of the latter codes to arm yourself fully, then make a thorough investigation of the planet, mapping it as you go along. Then restart the game, knowing what to expect. In addition to the codes mentioned in the *Strategy* sections, others you should check out are:

egBA ?vb? 2Xr8 5fP9 jW08 (letter O) vLPk Q0Y6 (letter O) nW25 (end)
j7hs EHvs d68o 9WKr qn08 (letter O) mS1x (one) tn2j p11m (letter l, letter l) (end)
Sg6N rsNL MVeJ qATJ vVx1 (one) tUeS gFGL cURF (the last of the trio gives you three Keys!)

If you want to start out with even more power, here are the codes you should use:

6E!B XsqE wzBE WscD YaVZ qwQb ehDS
Bcb? (end) AaWc 30Gj 63l(that's "el")q Ym0h
D1(that's "one")8! k!5c gPLw Ha4c (end)

There's one more code you can use, just for
fun: type in TGL, punch in only spaces for the
rest of the code, and get a load of what happens!

Rating: This is a true space odyssey, with much
to discover and many places and ways to defend yourself. And rarely has the graphic
potential of the NES been used to such eye-
popping advantage!

    Challenge: A
    Graphics: A
    Sound Effects: B

CHAPTER FIFTEEN

HYDLIDE

Type: Fantasy quest.

Manufacturer: FCI, under license from Nintendo.

Objective: So, you think Captain Kirk of *Star Trek* is the only bold adventurer named Jim? Not so! Jim is also a brave young knight who dwells in Fairyland. When the demon Boralis transforms Princess Ann into three fairies and hides her in different parts of the realm, Jim sets out to save her and defeat the fiend.

Layout: The screen is an overhead view, and scrolls both horizontally and vertically.

Hero: Jim sets out in full armor, and can collect eight different weapons as he journeys about. These are listed in the instructions and discussed below. Hits from enemies weaken Jim (indicated as a bar on the "Life" portion of the screen). Jim also acquires strength by gaining Experience (see *Scoring*). There are five different kinds of Magic, discussed in the *Strategy* sections below.

Enemies: There are 19 different kinds of enemies, all of whom are described in the instructions.

Menu: There's only the one-player game, though you can select two different speeds of gameplay.

Scoring: Each time Jim defeats a monster, his Experience grows and he becomes more powerful (indicated by a bar on the "Exp" portion of the screen). Otherwise, as he plays, Jim collects weapons and magic, not points.

Beginner's Strategy: The key to getting anywhere in *Hydlide* is to learn where all the Weapons are hidden and to amass the passwords that will enable you to tap those Weapons in succeeding games. See, the big problem with this cartridge is that when you lose a life, the game ends; no 1-Ups, no continue. You're just flat-out dead. So you need the codes.

Finding the necessary items and seriously getting the game under way can be a time-consuming ordeal. Some of you may want only a one- or two-weapon start; others may want a full arsenal to begin the game. Thus, here are the codes that will give you successive weapons and magic.

1. 798BLNR7L7BDHN75: Magic Vase and Cross
2. K2GN9PDH08MPQ580 (those are "zeroes,"

not "O's"): Magic Vase, Cross, and Turn (which causes monsters to do an about-face and leave you alone)

3. BH3H6PDB79PN8HM3: same as above, plus Fireball

4. 56BM5H8HM5BDHK11 (that's "one-one"): above, plus Eternal Lamp

5. KGTLMP8DDB0KQLL6 (that's a "zero"): above, though you're in a different locale

6. DDXGLKXHQ869RTG6: above, plus Secret Key

Advanced Strategy: The following codes will arm you for deeper penetration into the kingdom:

7. 8DKKDHQ5H935R4D0 (that's "zero"): above, in a different locale

8. RDVMMGV6Q7WHWDM6: above, plus Sword of the Brave

9. JGPMHNX8L9YGP6B5: above, different locale

10. BGJM3VRQ88RGGL50 (that's "zero"): above, plus one of the three Jewels

11. H48P7BKQG5WPKN00 ("zero zero"): above, different locale

12. XHPBJBPPB1K5KJM4 (that's "one," not "I"): above, plus Ice

13. ZBKKJKTLD9BBKLR7L and N49P89JN-H2HD7M11 ("one-one") same as above, different locales

14. V5YMN8VJJBH52BN7: above, plus Wave

15. 9BLGBPRKB9NPDR31 ("one"): same as above, different locale

There are still a few other items you'll need to obtain—for example, Flash and additional

Jewels—before you can start your Fairy hunt in earnest. However, when you have those, go to the Wasp trees (to get there, go to the site where code number 15 brings you . . . though obviously not using that code, or you'll lose the Flash and additional Jewels). From there, the directions are as follows: go right, right, right, down by the left side of the moat, down (into the hole), up through the maze to the next hole, down, down and out the left, left and up, right, right, down, down. Here, start hitting up on the trees, one at a time. Wasps will swarm out; since you're not anxious to be stung, duck down into the screen below, wait a few seconds, then go back up. Repeat this procedure several times with a number of trees. Finally, you'll hit one that'll give you the Fairy.

Go back to where you started the Fairy quest, and go right, right, and up to the Moving Trees. The same technique employed with the Wasps must be repeated here for another Fairy. One of the Moving Trees won't hurt you when you push up, but will give you the second Fairy.

Next on the agenda: killing the twin Wizards to obtain the third Fairy. These purple sorcerers are hanging around near the Moving Trees (if you want to check out their terrain, use code PBPKKJKM68RD6VG2). They'll be on the screen directly below you. In order to get the third Fairy, you must kill *both* sorcerers with one shot of Wave. Moreover, this must be done from the side, since Waves only work horizontally. Scoot down, blast them, and the third Fairy will be yours. The trio of sprites will then flutter over, pick you up, and fly you to the castle where you must face the guardian Dragon (with Flash) and the dangers therein.

If you want to start the game with most of the weapons as well as the Wasp-land Fairy, use the password Y9VNHNLHH9XD8RL6. If you want to start with a bunch of the Weapons, Wasp and Moving Tree Fairies, use T9V8GBVQ83X9JBN5. If you want to start with a hefty arsenal and all three Fairies (cheater!), type in H4QMLBQNH7B6BN73.

Always remember that if you need to recover your strength before getting to Boralis's castle, you can hide in clumps of foliage, where you're invisible to monsters.

Par: You should be able to get as far as obtaining the first two Fairies without using any of the codes above.

Training Tips: The fighting doesn't require much agility—simply the right tools for the right job. The only real preparation you can do is to make a map as you go along.

Rating: This game tries hard to be like the two Link adventures; it has that same look and theme. In some ways it succeeds (the game is complex, with a sprawling terrain); in other ways it fails (until you reach the castle, the monster fights are pretty dull).

Challenge: B
Graphics: C
Sound Effects: C (Someone's been listening to John Williams's "Indiana Jones March.")

CHAPTER SIXTEEN

MEGA MAN II

Type: Science fiction quest/shoot-'em-up.

Manufacturer: Capcom, under license from Nintendo.

Objective: The scurvy scientist Dr. Wily is back, hoping to conquer the world. But before he can do that, the superhero Mega Man attacks Skull Castle, intending to defeat Wily and his villainous servants.

Layout: The screen scrolls both horizontally and vertically, depending upon the level.

Hero: Created by Dr. Light, our pal Mega Man has many of Light's gizmos at his disposal, most notably the Levitation Platform for vertical movement, the Jet Sled for horizontal flight, and the Wall-Walking Platform for climbing (you guessed it!) walls. As for weapons, he starts off with a simple cannon, but can obtain the more powerful weapons of the major menaces (see *Enemies*) and use them against subsequent foes.

Enemies: Before he reaches the innards of Skull Castle and faces Wily, the magnificent Mega Man must mix it up with the major menaces Bubbleman, Airman, Quickman, Heatman, Woodman, Metalman, Flashman, and Crashman; and you thought he had it rough in the first game! There are also plenty of lesser pains in the neck, many of whom are discussed below.

Menu: Players can play alone or take the part of Mega Man on alternating turns. Two players cannot play at once. However, there are two difficulty levels, which determine how relentless your opponents will be.

Scoring: You earn points and energy for defeating foes; the easier the enemies (like the Air Gremlins and Prop-Tops), the lower the scores for beating them.

Beginner's Strategy: Not only is it important to know how to bash your way through the realms of each major villain, you have to know the best order in which to tackle them. Since some of the weapons you'll acquire work best against certain villains, here's the sequence you should follow: Airman, Crashman, Metalman, Heatman, Bubbleman, Woodman, and Flashman.

Here, in turn, are the key points to getting through the strongholds of each villain.

Airman: This is a horizontal level. The giant floating heads known as Air Tikis are the first challenge you'll encounter here. They *look* dangerous, with their Batmanlike ears, but never fear: just wait until the ears go down, then hop on top of their heads and continue to the right. When the swarming, purple Air Gremlins approach, don't destroy them until they're over the Tikis, so you can collect the energy residue. Moving right, you'll confront the Lightning Lords, who'll come flying in from the left, disappear into the clouds, then turn and attack you. As their name implies, these fiends in their cloud chariots fling bolts of lightning at you. Obviously, you should try to destroy them as soon as they appear behind you. Failing that, you've got problems. Since you'll be on narrow platforms and won't have much room to maneuver from side to side, you'll have to leap to avoid their bolts, and launch your own fire at the heads of the red-armored rowdies. When you defeat one, you can steal his chariot and ride it toward the next challenge. Next up on the right: the Fan Fiends, which fire powerful winds from their voluminous bellies. You'll be on girder-like platforms, and the trick here is to use these to keep from being blown from the sky. Approach the chubby windbags; in some cases you can jump up and fire at them, be blown back, and still land on a platform. In other cases, if they're on a platform higher than yours, you can use the left edge of their "girder" as a shield to lessen the impact of their winds. When you finally meet Airman, the key to beating him is to jump over his blasts of air and shoot him before he launches more. When you beat him, you'll acquire his powerful Air Shooter.

Crashman: On this level you'll spend brief spells in both a horizontal and vertical mode. Vertically, you'll face the Conveyor Belt, which requires no strategy other than the obvious: precise jumping and shooting. You'll also have to deal with Hard Hat Hooligan, whose headgear is impervious to your weapons. To beat him you must leap up to a platform, fire at Hooligan's vulnerable parts when he "tips" his hat to fire, then jump back down in case you missed and Hard Hat gets off another round. When you reach the darker section of the vertical tunnel, you should be alert for both an extra life (a.k.a. a 1-Up) and an Energy Canister, both of which will be found here (the Jet Sled will make the search easier). Next up is a horizontal delight: a showdown with the Prop-Tops, springy little creeps with propellers on their heads. Avoid them by dodging from side to side (leaping up is dangerous, since they do it higher and better), and shooting them as soon as they settle. When you reach the end of the horizontal passage, you'll face Crashman. Fight him by staying out of range of his attack and moving in between salvos. If you get too close at the wrong time, you're going to be Mega mush. Upon winning, you'll obtain Crash Bombs, which can be used to destroy foes . . . and certain walls.

Metalman: Transportation in this mostly horizontal realm is achieved by riding more Conveyor Belts. There's no strategy, per se, for moving from one to the other of these; only by playing can you get the feel for them. Until, that is, you meet the Metal Munchers. These spiked plates descend from the ceiling and will crush you unless you head to the right with carefully timed moves. No strategy needed, except for wide-open eyes and speed. Continuing on, you'll encounter wormlike Screws which move through the air ahead of you. Shoot them for Energy Canisters. Next on the menu are Gear Clowns, imps who ride rolling gears. Don't try to attack the Clowns themselves, at first; shoot the Gears out from under them, and then tackle the foul fools. Once you're beyond them, you'll have to fight Metalman. Put down Crash Bombs to penetrate his metal hide—and jockey hard to stay out of the way of his Metal Blades. These can be flung in eight different directions, so stay on the move!

Heatman: This adventure is mostly horizontal, and the Jet Sled is an indispensible tool for the novice player. Otherwise, getting through the initial stage of this level is accomplished by leaping from Block to Block. Problem is, these supports are only on screen for 2 short seconds. When you get to the vertical section of Heatman's home, you'll need Crash Bombs to get through the otherwise impenetrable section of floor. Just be careful you aren't clocked by the Spinning Spools, which whiz by and try to knock you into the pits that litter the landscape. This nemesis is most susceptible to the Air Shooter (which you've already collected, right?). When you return to horizontal travel you'll have to confront Heatman, a dude who possesses lethal Atomic Fire. The felon is vulnerable when he is in his humanoid rather than flame form. Shoot when he's in the former shape; jump, run, and generally stay the heck out of his way when he's in his thermonuclear stage. Once you acquire the power yourself, you'll be ready for your next challenge.

Advanced Strategy: Despite his wimpy-sounding name, Bubbleman is anything but weak . . . as you'll find out if you manage to reach him. First up: a horizontal tunnel and relatively simple leaps from platform to platform. Keep in mind that the red ones fall away suddenly and will drop you to your doom if you linger even a *moment* on one of them. After the red platforms, you'll come to a long white one, and two smaller ones that lead down from the right. On the bottom-most of these, go to the left side and jump; the screen changes to vertical here, and you'll want to make sure you hit a platform instead of plunging into an abyss. Maneuver your way down until you're moving horizontally again. You'll face the huge Lantern Fish, who will spit Super Shrimp at you. These jet-propelled prawn can be leaped or shot. As for the metal fish, it can be destroyed using Metalman's· Metal Blade;

simply jump up and shoot the fish in the eye-ball on the stalk at the top of its head. As you proceed, you'll encounter Croacker (sic). These are big frogs (you'll also have to destroy little frogs, who are their familiars), rela-tively easy to destroy with your Mega Man Cannon. However, Croacker is on a platform, and you'll have to jump up to kill it. The dan-ger here is that mines are attached to the ceil-ing, and if you jump even a smidge too high, you're going to look like part of a Fourth of July celebration. More platforms follow your encounter with the tadpole terrors, after which you'll meet Bubbleman and his Bubble Lead: a medicine-ball-sized object that'll roll you flat. Stay well to the left of the fiend, where the ceiling is highest, and leap the Bubble Leads that come steamrolling toward you. When you alight, use Metal Blades to de-feat the villain.

Woodman: Ah! A pastoral setting. But don't be misled: this is the very unfriendly Silicon Jungle. In the woods section you'll be fighting such foes as the Robo-Rabbits and their Car-rot Bombs (you can't destroy these explosives, so don't waste your Cannonfire) and the Atomic Chickens. To defeat the hares you have to shoot them on sight; if they start launching Carrots, it'll be tough to get off a shot. If you're on a ledge and they're beneath you, press 'em flat with a Bubble Lead. Ditto the Chickens, though you can also avoid them easily if they're on a platform above you: sim-ply snuggle up close to the edge of the platform they're on, and they'll leap right over you. When you reach the vertical section of the jungle, you'll eventually face the Hot Dogs. These mechanical blue hounds are fireball breathers who will reduce you to a mass of slag. Jump up to avoid the tongue of connected fireballs, then blast the corrupt canine with Atomic Fire. Once past Dogland, you'll journey up a tunnel to a series of platforms where you'll be driven ape by Mecha-Monkeys: large, powerful, mechanical gorillas. These hang beneath the platforms, then leap up and beat your computer brains out. When you see one, stay where you are. Wait until they swing up, then step back and give 'em a taste of the Cannon. Bye-bye banana breath. You'll go down another vertical passage, then through another horizontal forest and face more foul fowl, after which it's hello to Woodman. Woodman flings Leaves that protect him and hurt you. Reduce your trunk-shaped nemesis to toothpicks by using Crash Bombs (to which the shield of Leaves is not immune), or time your regular Cannon shots so that they strike when the Leaves are down.

Flashman and *Quickman:* The next two levels will bring you face to face with a variety of foes. However, you'll be so well armed by now, these shouldn't present a problem. In the Flashman stage you'll fight giant, mechanical walkers; your Bubble Lead will leave them lame. In the Quickman phase you will only be able to stop the Force Beams using the Time Stopper you'll have obtained from

Flashman. Defeat Quickman by feigning cowardice: turn from him, head in the opposite direction, then stop abruptly and shoot him. Quickman may be fast, but this ploy slows him down.

When you finally reach Skull Castle, you'll be facing enemies (the winged fire dragon, a giant cyborg tank known as the Guts-Dozer, etc.) who will require all your weapons and defenses. Remember, no matter how formidable the foe looks, don't panic. They're not that difficult to defeat. With the Guts-Dozer, for example, simply wait until its fists are down—monsters won't be disgorged at you then—jump onto the edge of the tank, and shoot it in the face. When you enter the room where the crushing blocks come flying at you, dodge and shoot them, and then stand in the spot they vacated: blocks can't come at you from the same place twice. If all else fails, you have the power to stop time and fire a wide variety of projectiles. With the living creatures, always aim for the head, and use your Levitation Platform, Jet Sled, or Wall-Walking Platform when necessary.

And now for the really good news! If you're demolished anywhere in the game, you get passwords so you can continue. Here are codes that will get you past each of the level bosses and will leave you armed with their powers:

Airman: A1, C145, D135, E13
Crashman: A1, C45, D1235, E14

> *Metalman: A2, B1, C25, D124, E14*
> *Heatman: A2, B135, C2, D124, E4*
> *Bubbleman: A1, C4, D1235, E124*
> *Woodman: A1, C34, D235, E124*
> *Flashman: A2, C25, D1234, E12*
> *Quickman: A2, B15, C2, D124, E14*

Par: If you reach the end of the Heatman stage, consider yourself a very good player.

Training Tips: So much of your success in this game is going to depend upon your leaping skills, you'd be wise to practice these. And the best place to do so is by opting to go right to the Heatman stage, where the Conveyor Belts leave little room for error.

Rating: What we said about *Mega Man* in the first book is true about *Mega Man II*. There's a great deal of terrain to explore (though less so than in the first game), but once you know it, some of the fun goes down the drain. Still, that'll take a while—and besides, fighting the baddies will never get boring.

> *Challenge:* B+ (tougher than the first game)
> *Graphics:* B— (crummier than the first game)
> *Sound Effects:* C (no better than the first game)

CHAPTER SEVENTEEN

MONSTER PARTY

Type: Horror shoot-'em-up.

Manufacturer: Bandai, under license from Nintendo.

Objective: While returning home from a baseball game, young Mark is met by Bert, a dragonlike creature from another world. Bert needs help: his home planet, the Dark World, has been overrun by evil monsters. Armed only with a baseball bat, Mark agrees to do what he can. As an added bonus, he is given the power to "fuse" with Bert and take wing at certain points during his journey through the insidious realm.

Layout: The screen scrolls horizontally, except for level seven, which scrolls vertically. There are eight levels, and a final one-on-one confrontation with the leader of the evil monsters, the Dark World Master.

Hero: Mark can walk, jump, and club monsters. Most monsters also fire some kind of projectiles; Mark can hit these back at them—generally, the fastest way to destroy a wicked alien. As Mark cracks Monsters' skulls with their own weapons or his Bat, some of the dead creatures leave behind Hearts, which boost the reading on Mark's Life Meter; and Capsules, which enable him to fuse with Bert for anywhere from 40 seconds to two minutes (depending upon the level reached and additional Capsules he may gulp down while in Bert form). As Bert, Mark can fly and fire powerful twin ray-bolts. Grabbing Mystery Items (indicated by a "?") left behind by deceased monsters gives you points or extra energy. In each level of Dark World, Mark must also obtain a Key from one of the boss monsters. Otherwise, he can't leave that level. As for the controls, there's one special trick you can perform with the NES Advantage: hold down the button to jump.

Enemies: Mark's enemies are discussed in the instruction booklet and also below. Boss monsters (from one to three of them on each level) live only behind doors in the realm. Be warned: since Mark can retrace his steps anywhere on any level, if you leave a screen and return, all the monsters (save for the bosses) will return. This can be good if you need Hearts, though: kill creatures again to collect more!

Menu: There's only the one-player game.

Scoring: Mark earns a wide range of points for clubbing monsters. He also earns 100 points for batting back their projectiles . . . even if he misses the monster.

Beginner's Strategy: Here's a level-by-level combat guide to each part of the Dark World.

Entrance: Go into the first door and kill the bubble-spitting Man-Eating Plant. You can accomplish this best by going to its right, leaping up onto the edge of the pot, and batting its stalk. You can also just stand in the center of the room and bat its bubbles back at it. There's an invisible platform to the far right in the room; you can stand there too, if you wish, and hit bubbles back. (The platform has no other purpose.) It'll take eleven whacks of the Bat to kill the plant. Claim the "?" and leave. Atop the next tall stone structure you'll kill a monster which will give you a Fuse. In the next room you'll find a dead Giant Spider. However, don't just turn and leave: slay the Fly circling it. You'll get another "?". After the green tower, watch out for Wolves and Walking Eyes (stay on top of the structures to avoid them both, or fight them for Hearts). Enter the door in the purple building to fight Pumpkin-Ghost. Wage the battle thusly: stand still over the last two digits of your score and hit the phantasm's skirt as it passes overhead; bat or dodge the mini-pumpkins it spits out at you. Claim the Key, pass the next two doors (the rooms are empty), and leave by the next door.

Dungeon: Climb the first big Ladder to the top and enter the door. Go right up to the Medusa and club her (the snakes she spits won't present much of a problem). Get the "?" and go back down the Ladder to the second floor. Get a Fuse at the end and go to the top level, then down the Ladder, to the left, down the Ladder to the bottom level, then head right. The room on top is empty, so avoid it. Continue heading right. When you can't go anymore, climb the Ladder to the second floor. Head left, up the Ladder, to the top. Get a Fuse here, go right, down the Ladder, and left to the door. To triumph over the Shrimp Attack, hit the monster in the back, duck when it reaches the side and turns, then follow it again. The creature will transform, in turn, into what looks like a giant onion ring, then a shredded wheat on a stick. Keep repeating the procedure until it dies. Get the "?" and go right when you leave. Head up the Ladder, down the next Ladder, left, down the Ladder, and right on the bottom level (the door on the second level is empty). Go up the big Ladder to the top, head left, and enter the doorway on top. The Haunted Well spits big, lethal Coins at you; bat the top of the Well to beat it, jumping up between Coin attacks. Collect the Key, go back down the Ladder to the right. Climb the big Ladder at the wall, go down the next big Ladder, up the next big one, stay on the top to the end, then climb down and enter the drain. Leave the level.

Cave: The monsters on this level are bigger

and more powerful than before. As you begin, blue Stalactites will fall. These aren't much of a problem to Mark, since you'll have time to move and dodge them. However, if you become Bert and are flying, there will be much less time to get out of the way. Edge past this section, then ignore the first door (it's empty). The second door at the far base of the small mountain contains Bull Man. Stand over the word "Round," swinging your Bat at the Bull Man and his tiny Bull Kids. They'll all die easily. Leave and get a Fuse from the Bat-Monster you'll encounter. Fly low to avoid the Stalactites. Enter the door at the three-tiered peak: inside, lie on the paws of the Sphinx and shoot the Mummy. Again, nothing too difficult in there. The next door under the steps is empty, as is the door under the following set of steps. After the second empty door you'll face a Bat-Monster in a narrow corridor; kill it for a Fuse. Enter the next door and fight the Giant Spider and its flurry of Strands by flying over the creature and shooting when you're behind it. Get the key from the dead arachnid and go right to the exit.

Castle Ruins: Slip under the moving Block and kill the Scorpion. The door on top is empty, so forget about it. Bat projectiles back at the second Scorpion (on the Block), and get a Fuse. Go right, and at the edge of the ledge (across from which the Scorpion is shooting down), fly up, go left, and enter the room. Simply go up to the Giant Samurai and hack at its legs; get a new Fuse. Go right on the bottom and enter the door. There's a Giant Cat here, and it throws miniature cats at you. Go to the right, behind the fantastic feline, jump up to the crate and bat the kitty on the head. Get an energy "?" and leave. Go left and up to the top level. Get a Fuse from the Scorpion behind the moving Block. The next door is empty; fly to the door at the top and fight the Punk Rocker whose notes can kill you. Just fly over the musician and hit his back; he'll die faster than a bad record. Leave, and you'll come to a section where there's a Scorpion on top and a moving Block in the middle. Bat one of the Scorpion's projectiles at the moving Block to destroy it. Leave the Castle Ruins.

Advanced Strategy: Here are the remaining levels.

Lake: The rooms here are in Tree Trunks; you'll have to look carefully to spot them. Stand on the second rock from the right and hit the Sea Serpent as it nears. The first room is empty. Go along, killing monsters for Hearts; the first Skeleton Fish gives you a Fuse. The next door is empty, and the third pits you against the easiest foe in the game: the Living Dead. Enter the room and stand still; the zombies will come toward you and dance . . . and keep on dancing until they turn to dust. You do nothing. Leave, and fly to the right, killing monsters for energy. Enter the door in the air. The Mad Javelin Man is here (the keenest-looking monster in the game, by the way). Fly up, ducking his spears, and blast him repeatedly in the face. You'll be rewarded with the Key. The next two rooms are empty, and the third is your way out of the level.

Haunted House: Because this is a looooong maze, many players find this the most difficult level of all. There are really two phases. First, finding the room with the Key (there are more doors here than in the Empire State Building!), and second, finding the exit from the level. To make matters worse, there's a steady stream of Ectoplasm (ghost goo) raining down from above. This must be batted, jumped, or ducked under as you proceed. Always keep in mind that the easiest way to kill any foe is to club Ectoplasm at them; one hit and they're goners! To get to the Key room: enter the door at the right wall. Go right in the door at the wall, right again, and fight the giant Table (yes . . . a giant, living Table), enter the door at the wall, go right and drop down the pit. Fight the living Pants, then go right to the door at the wall, right again to the next door at the wall. Fight more Pants and go right to the door at the wall, then right to the door at the next wall. Enter the next door to the right, go right into the door at the wall, and you're in the Key room. The Chameleon Man is actually four masks that blend in with the mottled background. It's a terrific foe, difficult to see until it moves; hit any one of the masks and all are hurt. Just try not to be pinned in the corner by all four, or you'll be one dead earthling. Leave the room and retrace your steps to the beginning. Be warned, though: if you don't get a Fuse along the way, you won't be able to fly up the pit again. In that case, you'll have to map your own route back through the Haunted House. Keep in mind, though, that if you die, although you can continue at that level, you'll lose the Key and will have to obtain it again. Once you're back where you started, here's how to get to the exit: enter the door on the far left, go right to the pit, jump down, head right, enter the door at the wall, go right to the door at the wall, go right again to the door at the wall, fight the Pants, go right to the door at the next wall, and go right again to the door at this wall. Go in the next door to the right. Fight the living Chair in the giant room, then go right into the door at the wall. Drop down the pit, fight the Table, and go right to the door at the wall. Now, fight the Table and enter the second door you encounter. Go into the next door on the right, to the door at the left wall, fight the giant Chair, then leave the level via the door at the right.

Tower: When you reach the second floor, get two Hearts and a "?" from the monsters here. On the third floor get a Fuse from the monster on top. There's a door on the left, with a Giant Caterpillar inside. Fly over it and blast it when it's at the right side of the screen. Get a "?" and climb to the next screen. Several floors later there's a door on the top right; it's empty (actually, it says "Come again," which doesn't mean a darn thing). Three floors later is another door, on the bottom left; it's the Entrance to Hell, and you must fight the Grim Reaper. Demons will circle you as you fly and hit the Reaper's face. (You'll get a Fuse on this floor, which is important: if you don't have it, you'll have to jump up to hit the tall Reaper's skeletal face, which is difficult because of the demons). Get the Key and leave. The next door is four floors up, and it's another "Come again" room. The next floor has a door on the upper left, and the third "Come again" (all is not lost: you'll get a Fuse on this floor). Don't bother with the next two doors you encounter; the third will let you out of the level.

Heaven's Castle: This is a starlit realm resting on a bed of Clouds, a world of roaming Witches, flying candles, and Constellations that fire Stars at you. There are seven doors on this level. Go right, to the first, but don't go in: it's empty. Go to the far right of the Cloud that it's on, slide off, and get under the edge of the Cloud. The Big Dipper will form overhead; bat its Stars back at it. Get one Star in the bowl of the Dipper and it's history. Now, get back up on the Cloud, go left, destroy Candles for Hearts, go right to the edge of the Cloud, turn left again, kill the same Candles and collect more Hearts. Repeat this procedure until the Clouds run dry. Then, head *left,* to a cathedral. Enter and fight the Giant Dragon. This is the toughest creature in the game. Stand on the floor (even if you've Fused), between your score and the word "Round." The Dragon will uncoil and come down at you. Shoot at its head. It'll swoop down from the direction of the score; when it does, jockey over to "Round." When it swings up and comes down at you again from "Round," inch over to the score, turn, and fire again at its head. Repeat this until the creature dies. When you've defeated it, go right again. Pass the first door and enter the second room to battle the Hand Creature. This is actually a multi-armed statue which sits still while it fires stuff at you. Simply go to the far right and shoot it in the back. Death will come quickly. The third room is empty, although if you duck inside and come out again, the Constellation outside will vanish. You'll get a Fuse right after this room. The fourth room is occupied by Snake Man, who is really a giant, crawling head. Leap it when it charges, shoot the back of the head, wait until it turns and charges again, leap once more, and so on. Get the Key here and obtain a Fuse right after you leave. The next room is empty, and the one after that is the entrance to the castle that is the abode of the Dark World Master.

Master: The guy looks intimidating. His head fills the room, with massive teeth on the bottom and huge eyes on top. All kinds of nasties fly from the Master's mouth; if you're Mark, chances are good you're going to die here. If you've Fused (and there's no reason you shouldn't have), hover midscreen on the left and shoot at the Master's *nose*. When you've blasted this off, the Master will die.

As a reward for your efforts, Bert gives Mark a gift: a lovely princess. When he returns to earth, however, she becomes a horrible monster; Mark screams and—surprise!—he awakes. It was all a nightmare. Just then there's a knock on the door and (you guessed it!) in walks Bert. The game begins anew.

Par: A good player shouldn't have any trouble until level six. Par score for each level is approximately 70,000 points.

Training Tips: Have a look at all the levels before you play. Codes that will allow you to access each level are:
1. Just plug in the cartridge!
2. CnD o4o 3sH
3. RvX "HS in4 (that's a "close" quote)
4. tvL G-B 6me or 1AI GqO 77W
5. 1yF 84O 77D or JuE piV "D6 ("close" quote)
6. UtB DGC ,OJ or 93W zt. y7,
7. sfh sQV F9B
8. a!B BOL ?hX

There's no code to go directly to the Master. You can only get to him by winning level eight.

Rating: Exciting gameplay, and good variety from level to level make this a very rewarding cartridge. It's good family fun, since it won't scare anyone and the lower levels are good for young players.

    Challenge: B+

Graphics: B— (Some monsters are fuzzily detailed, and you can't always tell what they are.)

Sound Effects: A (There are *incredible* howling wind sounds on level six.)

CHAPTER EIGHTEEN

NINJA GAIDEN

Type: Martial arts combat.

Manufacturer: Tecmo, under license from Nintendo.

Objective: Ken is the head of the Hayabusa clan and keeper of the legendary Dragon sword. When he's defeated by the forces of the evil Jaquio, his son Ryu must go to America and, armed with the Dragon sword, avenge the defeat of his father.

Layout: The screen scrolls primarily from side to side, with a small amount of vertical action. There are six different "Acts" with a total of 20 different scenes between them. One unique aspect of this game is that you can double back and return to a screen you've already left, in case you want to kill someone you may have missed. You don't have to learn your way around the realm: when the game wants you to change directions, you simply won't be able to continue any longer the way you were headed (for example, there'll be a wall in the way and you'll have to go up).

Hero: Ryu's basic powers are jumping, clinging to walls, and bouncing off walls, like a wrestler tossed against the ropes. As he travels, he can also acquire power-up items. These are discussed in the instruction booklet, and also in the strategy sections below. Just one pointer now: the Invincible Fire-Wheel only lasts 10 seconds, so when you get it, rush ahead.

Enemies: In addition to the malicious Jaquio, who wants to conquer the world and lives in the "evil temple," you have to face "the Malice Four," the bosses of each level. There are actually five bosses, but who's counting? These are discussed below.

Menu: There is only the one-player game.

Scoring: You earn points (for example, Spiritual Strength) for slaying enemies, and lose points each time you use a weapon (see instruction for amounts). You also play against a timer. If you don't complete your level by the time it runs out, you lose a life.

Beginner's Strategy: This is one of those games where knowing the layout isn't going to help as much as having reflexes like the Karate Kid. This is especially true in Act V, when the villains swarm around you like gnats; literally, since some of the evil Ninjas fly! Still, there *are* things you can do to make your journey less dangerous. For one thing, always keep an eye out behind you: Dogs run at you from both directions. For another, there's a way to use the Windmill Throwing Star even more effectively than it was intended. When thrown, this weapon returns to you like a boomerang. When it comes back, *don't* catch it. Leap as you continue in the direction you were headed, and let the Star pass under you each time it comes back. By zipping back and forth, it'll cut a safety zone for you on either side. Finally, a skill you should learn to master is rapid wall climbing. This works best with the NES Advantage joystick: press it fast in a series of counterclockwise jerks while rapidly punching the A button. You'll climb faster than if you simply follow the climbing guide in the instruction booklet.

Anyway, the foes are pretty easy in Act I. Except for watching out for the Dogs, you shouldn't have a problem here. When you reach the Barbarian boss, many players opt to hit the kingpin, climb the wall and hang there, run down and stab again when the brute is open, and so forth. This is effective, but time consuming. All you have to do is run at him immediately (he's on the right side), give him a taste of your sword, back up to avoid his blade, dart over and hit him again, back up when he swings, run in again, and so on. He'll die quickly.

Act II is also not too tough. The first time you have to play II/2, however (Death Valley), here's something to remember: when you leap from a tower to a platform guarded by a Ninja (especially the first one), you *must* land on the very edge of the platform (the edge nearest you). Otherwise, he'll kill you before you can kill him. Also, watch out for the kneeling Gunner-Ninjas on some of these platforms. If the platform rests on a wall, simply jump to the wall and cling to it until the shooting stops, then climb up and kill him. If the platform rests on a pillar, get over there *at once*, before he starts shooting. Late in the II/2 stage you'll no longer be able to kill everyone who's running at you. You'll have to leap over some of the Ninjas to slaughter those beyond them, then turn and kill the ones you jumped. Bomberhead, the boss in II/3, is also no big deal to kill. Leap over him using the Jump & Slash Technique (see instruction booklet) and he'll go down. You can acquire this power by cutting a Lantern found shortly after climbing a tower in II/2.

Act III isn't much more difficult than the first two acts. You'll get the Windmill Throwing Star early in the round, which makes things easier. A few things to which you should pay particular attention are these: when you come upon Ninjas standing close together, wait until they wander apart, then jump between them and kill them. Also, charge the Gunners at once. Time, now, becomes more important than before, and you don't want to have to hang around until they stop shooting. When you meet the boss, a tougher nut than the other two, go immediately to the center boulder. The boss will leap from one side of the screen to the other; you, too, should jockey slightly to the left or right of the boulder as the boss is leaping, and stab him when he lands. You may take a few hits here, but you'll still come out victorious.

As you go through Acts I through III, you'll find the power-ups and bonuses in the following order. Some are on upper levels, some lower; all are listed as they appear when you proceed through the rooms. A few landmarks have been provided (for example, climb two floors) for quick reference during gameplay.

Act I/1: Power Boost, Power Boost, Power Boost, Star, Blue Bonus (500 points), Power Boost, Power Boost, Red Bonus (1000 points), Blue Bonus, Fire-Wheel, Jump & Slash, Power Boost, Fire-Wheel, Time Freeze, Blue Bonus, Power Boost, Windmill, Power Boost.

Act II/1: Power Boost, Power Boost, Power Boost, Star, Red Bonus, Fire-Wheel, Red Bonus, Power Boost, Power Boost, Windmill, Red Bonus, Blue Bonus, Power Boost (climb up to second level to continue), Power Boost, Blue Bonus, Jump & Slash, Red Bonus, Power Boost, Star, Blue Bonus (climb two floors to continue), Red Bonus, Blue Bonus, Star, Power Boost.

Act II/2: Power Boost, Power Boost, Blue Bonus, Star, Power Boost (descend a floor), Restore Life, Fire-Wheel, Power Boost, Power Boost, Blue Bonus (ascend a level), Power Boost, Power Boost, Blue Bonus, Jump &

Slash, Power Boost, Fire-Wheel, Power Boost, Blue Bonus, Red Bonus.

Act III/1: Power Boost, Power Boost, Power Boost, Time Freeze, Star, Red Bonus, Power Boost, Fire-Wheel, Power Boost, Restore Life, Blue Bonus.

Act III/2: Power Boost, Power Boost, Blue Bonus, Windmill, Power Boost, Red Bonus, Power Boost, Fire-Wheel, Blue Bonus, Red Bonus, Power Boost, Power Boost, Blue Bonus, Windmill, Power Boost.

Advanced Strategy: The first scene of Act IV is a lot busier than anything you've experienced to date, but no one here is very difficult to kill. When you hit level two, stay on top as much as possible, so the Ninjas don't drop their knives on you. When you reach the first pit, wait. Don't jump until the Bat flies over and past you. If you'd jump immediately, you'd have hit the creature and fallen to your death. On the third level, when you reach the first boxlike objects, climb up carefully to get the power-up item hanging just below the top. Claim it before attacking the Ninjas here. You'll be using your bouncing skills on this level more than ever before, so make sure you know how to ricochet between walls before playing this level. When you reach the boss, you're in for a surprise: there are two of them, both vicious demon Dogs . . . but one of 'em is a fake who can't be killed. When you enter the room, immediately stab the figure on the left. This is the real one. Rush to the right, which is where it'll be hopping in just a moment, and attack when it gets there. Stay on the right and stab at it whenever it's within reach. (Some players prefer to stay in the middle. This is okay if you lose track of which hound is real and which is the fake. Otherwise, stay with the one you have to kill, and don't be distracted by the other.)

In Act V start by using the same pit strategy described in IV/1. Watch out for the disk-tossing Ninja lurking by the blue column; use the Windmill Throwing Star to take him out. Again, stay on top whenever possible to avoid the knife-dropping Ninjas. At approximately the 85-second mark you'll reach the edge of a vast pit; use the pit strategy again before jumping. In V/2 green Ninjas jump at you from offscreen on the top. Watch for them, and be ready to slow down or speed up to deal with them. (Fortunately, you'll get the Invincible Fire-Wheel early in the level, which will sizzle many of the rats as they leap at you.) This level also presents a unique problem involving the face of a cliff which may seem impassable. Naturally, it isn't. You'll be standing on a boxlike ledge when a big outcropping of rock looms in front of you, with a ledge beneath it. You can't jump to that lower ledge without plummeting to your death, so here's all you do: run straight off the ledge into the outcropping. Use it to bounce you back to the bottom of the boxlike ledge on which you were standing. Then bounce to the right, onto the ledge. Again: it's a right, left, right maneuver, fairly simple when you get the hang of it. Another way to cross is to jump up to the right and climb the rock while pressing the A button and jabbing left-right repeatedly on the controls. When Ryu reaches the top, let him fall. Miraculously, he'll land on the ledge. The second screen of level V/3 introduces the Flying Ninjas, who are easy to kill with a leap and stab. The Bats, though, continue to present a problem at the pits; they come in flocks, so you'll have to be careful here. Time your jumps, and be instantly on your guard when you reach the other side, since the Dogs tend to attack as soon as you alight. At the V/4 stage you can beat the boss by getting in close (though be careful, for his electric touch is death) and stabbing him *fast*. Stay in there and hack away, making fine adjustments in your position as Bloody Malth tries to cremate you.

Act VI is fast and murderous, a mix of everything you've had to face so far . . . and *then* some. The one key trouble area is located at approximately the 100-second level of VI/2, the green-crate area. You really have to rush through this part, or be reduced to Ninjaburger. Leap the first pit (first killing the enemy on the other side with the Windmill Throwing Star), then run and jump the second pit without hesitation, killing the Bat without stopping (dawdle, and you'll be overwhelmed). Then leap up to the cratelike object on top to avoid almost certain death on the ground. And you're going to need a *ton* of

Spiritual Strength to face the chief villain, so save up that power!

Here's a guide to which weapons and bonuses you'll find in the latter acts:

Act IV/1: Power Boost, Power Boost, Red Bonus, Blue Bonus, Jump & Slash, Windmill, One-Up, Power Boost, Fire-Wheel, Power Boost, Blue Bonus, Red Bonus. There's nothing from the time you begin climbing the large wall through the end of the level.

Act IV/2: Power Boost, Power Boost, Windmill, Power Boost, Power Boost, Power Boost, Fire-Wheel, Red Bonus, Blue Bonus, Power Boost, Power Boost, Star, Time Freeze (nothing until the end of the plateau), Windmill, Red Bonus, Restore Life, One-Up, Jump & Slash, Blue Bonus, Power Boost, Windmill.

Act IV/3: Fire-Wheel (top), Power Boost, Blue Bonus, Power Boost, Power Boost, Windmill, Red Bonus (climb), Windmill, Red Bonus, Power Boost, Restore Life, Fire-Wheel, Blue Bonus, Red Bonus (climb), Red Bonus, Windmill (top), Power Boost, Power Boost.

Act V/1: Power Boost, Star (top), Power Boost, Blue Bonus, Power Boost, Red Bonus, Windmill, Power Boost, Power Boost, Blue Bonus, Red Bonus, Fire-Wheel, Power Boost, Windmill, Restore Life, Red Bonus, Power Boost.

Act V/2 (power-ups become scarcer beginning with this level): Power Boost, Power Boost, Blue Bonus, Jump & Slash, Power Boost, Fire-Wheel (over the small ledge on the bottom), Red Bonus, Star, Power Boost, Fire-

Wheel, Blue Bonus, Red Bonus, Windmill, Power Boost (climb two screens), Restore Life, Blue Bonus, Red Bonus, Power Boost.

Act V/3: Power Boost, Power Boost, Power Boost, Fire-Wheel, Red Bonus, Power Boost, Blue Bonus (ascend wall), Star, One-Up (top), Red Bonus, Blue Bonus, Fire-Wheel (ascend), Power Boost, Windmill, Star (ascend), Fire-Wheel, Blue Bonus, Power Boost (ascend), Fire-Wheel, Windmill, Power Boost.

Par: You should be earning 50,000 points by the end of Act II, and an average of 35,000 points for each complete act thereafter.

Training Tips: Try to get through without resorting to any of the ultimate weapons. That'll certainly sharpen your acrobatic skills, if nothing else.

Rating: As fighting games go, this one's a winner, and the bouncing aspect of your hero is especially wild!

Challenge: A—

Graphics: B (The animation is good, the scenery so-so . . . except for an incredible panorama that appears, unheralded, at the end of Act IV, scene 1.)

Sound Effects: B+ (There's a great drum beat under the action.)

CHAPTER NINETEEN

SKATE OR DIE

Type: Skateboarding contests.

Manufacturer: Ultra Software, under license from Nintendo.

Objective: Rodney Recloose is the owner of the Flesh 'N Asphalt Skateboard Shoppe, and the surrounding community is ruled by himself, his son Bionic Lester, and their gang—ruled because of their awesome skateboarding skills. As a newcomer in town, you want to carve off some turf of your own. To do so, you must prove that you're better on wheels than the reigning kings of street surfing.

Layout: Different screens have different views, either from the side, in which the screen is stationary, or from overhead, scrolling from bottom to top.

Hero: Your skateboarder has a variety of different moves, all of which are described in the instruction booklet. The one option that deserves special mention is the ability to play Regular Foot or Goofy Foot. This has no bearing on strategy, but simply means that you can work your skateboarder as if you were controlling a marionette *or* as if you were looking through the rider's eyes. The view doesn't change, but the way you work the controls does: in Regular Foot, for example, a left push sends the board to the left; the opposite is true in Goofy Foot.

Enemies: Poseur Pete, Aggro Eddie, and the aforementioned Bionic Lester are your opponents. Each has greater ability than the one before.

Menu: There are five different games from which to choose: Jam, in which you race down back streets and alleys, causing your opponents to crash into fences and manholes; Joust, in which you knock your opponent off his board; Downhill Race, a romp through the obstacle-filled countryside, in which you compete against the timer; and High Jump and Freestyle, both of which take place in a dish-shaped ramp. These two demand that you jump as high as possible and show off your moves, respectively. There's also a Compete All Street mode, in which you go directly from one match to the other. Up to eight players can enjoy *Skate or Die* on successive turns.

Scoring: You earn points and/or race against the clock, depending upon the match.

Beginner's Strategy: Taking the games from easiest to most challenging:

High Jump: If you have the NES Advantage or Max, you've already got the game in the bag: Turbo practically gives you wings. The important thing to remember is that if you fall, you score zippo—no matter how high your leap was. Since you gain speed (and height) by pumping the B button, you don't want your finger to cramp. Take a break while your skateboarder swings into the air on the left side, and begin pumping hard as he comes down and rides toward the right.

Freestyle: You'll do better if you do your maneuvering in the foreground. Your skateboarder has a habit of clipping the edge of the dish on the far side, right.

Joust: Each player has the Lance for a count of 5 on the timer, and then the weapon switches over. The pattern here is simple. When you're on the defensive, maneuver in a large, wide clockwise or counterclockwise circle. For example, if your opponent starts with the Lance, move your character to the near edge, skate down, come up the right side, ride to the back, come down the side and up the left, then come forward. That's a lot of territory for your enemy to cover. When you're on the offensive, keep to the center of the pool, moving in tight figure-eights up and down the sides. This pattern will give you the maximum coverage of the area where he'll be moving, and the best chance of intercepting him.

Advanced Strategy: The more difficult games should be played as follows:

Downhill Race: In order to obtain the highest scores, head to the right, following the zigzag road, and jump the Wall for 400 points. But be alert: there's another barrier dead-ahead. (If you start the game going left, cut across the grass to save time, then go off the Ramp for 200 points; land firmly, and you'll add another c-note to your score. You'll make better time but earn fewer points than you will on the right-hand route). Head diagonally to the left and scoot through the Pipe (you can't get through this unless you duck down), continue straight ahead and jump the Ramp for 200 points. If you avoided the Pipe and took the right-hand route, you'll come away with precious few points. Just below the island in the lake you'll find a Grate you can leap for 100 points. Just for the thrill of it, try leaping some of the smaller rock formations. While you're at it, see if you can make it across the lake!

Jam: This really requires some precision maneuvering—especially if you opt to go through the wooden gate (which you should, to stay clear of your adversary). If you fall here, though, you'll start up again on the outside. Obviously, you should try to get ahead of your opponent and either cut him off or squeeze him against a fence. It's worth sacrificing a few fractions of a second to do this in order to have a free field when it comes to smashing Bottles that line the route.

Par: A good player will be able to accomplish the following in each of the games:
High Jump: 8'6" with Turbo, 5'3" without
Freestyle: 6000 points
Downhill Race: 20 seconds, 9000 points
Jam: 40 seconds and 9000 points

Training Tips: This one's easy; go to the practice mode and don't leave until you're ready to take on the champs.

Rating: Not only is the variety of this cartridge impressive, but it's a good party game.
Challenge: B
Graphics: B (The scenery is good, and though the detail on the skateboarders could be better, the animation is quite good.)
Sound Effects: C+ (More rattling wheels and whistling wind, and less music would have been a big improvement.)

CHAPTER TWENTY

STRIDER

Type: Ninja slice-'em-up.

Manufacturer: Capcom, under license from Nintendo.

Objective: Strider is the name of a group of crack agents who specialize in difficult military maneuvers. The player takes the part of Hiryu, a retired Strider who is forced back into action when rogue Striders plot to use the mind-control machine Zain to conquer the world. In addition to shooting enemies and obtaining weapons (a.k.a. "Tricks"), you must locate Keys which open doors, and find and analyze Message Disks, acquiring information you'll need to complete the mission.

Layout: The screen scrolls horizontally, with occasional vertical passages. There are seven levels: six different countries plus the Red Dragon headquarters.

Hero: Hiryu begins with the ability to jump and duck, and is also armed with a blade known as the Cipher. As the game progresses he can also obtain deadlier Plasma Arrows, Spark Balls, Boots (red for climbing, yellow for attacking, blue for walking on water), the ability to slide (useful for getting past a series of leaping adversaries and a necessity for getting under low overhangs), and various Tricks (see instruction booklet and below) which improve everything from his health to his supply of Bullets.

Enemies: There are numerous (and nameless) warriors and tanklike robots which, for the most part, are easily defeated. The toughies are the likes of Badger, Kodiak, Dragon Friend, and Flash Blade (see below).

Menu: There's only the one-player game.

Scoring: There are no points or timer; you lose energy when you're hurt, or gain energy when certain defeated enemies leave behind Energy Capsules. There are two energy gauges: one for your general health, the other for your Trick powers.

Beginner's Strategy: Each of the countries you need to fight your way through is more or less the same; different scenery, but the same menaces and jumping/sliding/slashing techniques. The unique aspect of this game is that you won't finish a country before moving on to the next. For example, to complete Kazakh, you must get the Magnetic Boots, which are found in China. However, you can't get to China just yet. You must first read the two Data File disks in Kazakh which allow you to go to Egypt; from there you must go to Australia and Japan.

Without telling you exactly when to break off to switch countries (it'll be obvious: keep checking your Transfer screen, and make the switch when you're allowed), here are things to look out for in each country.

Kazakh: After picking your way through the complex, you'll eventually find an Idol room. There are many such rooms scattered throughout the game. You'll be attacked here by a boxlike device that circles the room, shooting at you. Duck its fire and slash at the midsection of the Idol; this will rid you of both. Once inside the complex, you'll find, in turn, two Data Files, a Key, and the Slide Trick. You won't be able to do more, however, without the Magnetic Boots. (When you have them, return to Kazakh and you'll eventually come to a sheer, red wall on the left, which must be climbed. Doing so, cross the ceiling; upon reaching the end of the ceiling, drop onto the platform below and continue. Your journey here is nearly at an end.)

Egypt: You'll begin here atop the Phantom Train. Stay on it and fight your way to the right. When you reach the pyramid, climb it and come down the other side. It's tough to brake and kill the guys there, so your best bet is to run down, leaping them as you go. As much as possible, stay out of the Elevators here: like pneumatic tubes, they'll zip you back over miles of terrain, forcing you to fight your way through all over again. It's a nifty effect to see . . . but only if someone else is playing. (Tell your little brother to go into one . . . then explain to your parents that you were only trying to help!)

Australia: Jump the Spikes here, which lie between the columns. If you fall in, you're dead. (You can use the Jump Trick to get out, if you have it . . . but that's a *huge* waste of Trick energy.) You won't be able to go far here without the fifth Key, which can be found in Los Angeles (see below).

Japan: The first enemy leaves an Energy Capsule when slain. Also, when you face the twin bird creatures, go at once to the sides of the screen, since they fire toward the middle.

China: To begin the level, jump down at the first big pit, avoiding the Elevators that came before. Enter the cavern and climb up the diagonal passages. Look here for the Attack Boots; go right, down the first Elevator, then left, down, right in the chamber (ducking behind blocks to avoid the moving spiked walls which come at you horizontally). Fight the enemy at the end, go down, right, then through a second moving wall room. Take the Elevator down, jump off the ledge on the right side; the Attack Boots are in the bottom left of the pit.

Africa: A jungle setting, you must cross a crocodile swamp (just wait till their heads go under), climb the tree branches (taking care not to fall on the deadly green spikes), head left, use Jump to get off the nestlike object (it sinks fast, and you'll need a big leap to get away), and keep climbing. Eventually you'll reach a complex with many of the nestlike falling platforms, as well as other foes. But there's nothing too difficult here. Attack the Fireball Spitter after each salvo of three Fireballs; the second such automaton leaves you an Energy Capsule. Watch out for the Idol Room.

There's also one other, unheralded stop you have to make in order to get the fifth Key: "Los Angeles." In order to get there, you have to read the sixth Data File. When you get to L.A., go right, duck the moving spiked walls, go down the third of the Elevators on the bottom, go left, fight the enemy, and enter the horizontal Elevator on the left. Continue left through the Cave, go down the Pit on the far left, jump the spikes as you head right, and stop at the Dome on the right. Smash it using your Cipher and/or Fire, then enter the room behind it and take the fifth Key. (The code that will save you the trouble of having to go through all this is BJAP NEAN ANMB.)

If you're having trouble with one or more countries and want to jump ahead, here are the codes that will allow you to do so . . . armed with a variety of weapons and other items (energy levels and various powers increase with each successive code):

BCJB BBNB NBAB: Kazakh, Egypt, Australia;
  Data File 1 and 2; Key 1
DGPD LDBD BDAD: Same plus Japan, Slide,
  Aqua Boots, Fire, Medical 1, and Data
  File 3
EIAE MEDE CEBE: Same plus Spark, Jump,
  and Data File 4
FJBF NGEF DFBF: Same plus Plasma Arrow
HLDJ PIGH GHCH: Same plus China
HLDJ DIGH GHGH: Same plus Magnet Boots
INKH EJHI HIJI: Same plus Warp and Keys
  2, 3, 4
BHAD NCAJ ABKB: Same plus Ground and
  Data File 5
OFNA KPNK NGKO: Same plus Africa,
  Medical 2, and Data File 6
OFNA MPNK NGMO: Same, plus Attack
  Boots
DMCC PGCP CPMD: Will bring you to Red
  Dragon headquarters, armed with all of
  above Tricks (except Attack Boots) plus
  Spark Ball and Medical 3

Advanced Strategy: Making your way through the
Red Dragon headquarters will require all
your skills and weapons. Go right, jump the
spikes, and use the Triangle Jump (see instruction booklet) to climb the Columns. Head
left to the Elevator, go up, right, leap the
spikes, and ascend the first Elevator (Kodiaks
attack when you emerge, so be alert!). Head
left, running from Column to Column, but
watch out: lasers above will begin shooting
down at you. If you set out immediately and

don't break your stride, you'll get through just fine. Slide under the overhead Column at the end, go up the right-most Elevator, and head right. Slide past the three Elevators, go through the door at the end (slashing the hound-thing that attacks just before you enter). You'll have to face Flash Blade here. When his swords are crossed, you can't hurt him. Wait until he jumps and spreads his arms, then get in close and slash him. He'll spin like a top. When he slows down, wait for him to open his arms again, then repeat. He'll die soon enough. If you've started from the room and a bonus item appears, don't back-track to pick it up; if you come back once you've gone to the door, Flash Blade will re-constitute and attack anew!

Leave the room and go right. Travel up the Elevator, go right, kill the robot, and go down the next three Elevators. Go left (not into the next Elevator below). When you see the Cipher hovering in the air, jump down. Beneath it is the Elevator you must take. After emerging from the Elevator, go right. You'll face the Dragon Friend here; attack using your Cipher and/or Plasma Arrows when he's still on the far side of the room. When he dies, go right, through the door, and battle the shark monster: rush to the right and get in your hits against this creature before it moves. Run left when it stirs and make attacks against it as you can. When it dies, go right, through the doors, and up the Elevator. Go left and use the Magnetic Boots to climb the wall. (A note about the Boots: they're a little disorienting, so pay attention. You have to press left to go up, down to duck, up to go down. Don't use the A button or you'll fall.) At the top, go up by taking a quick right, then going left. Pass through the door and go up the Elevator; on the right is the system you must destroy. Just kill the enemy there with the Cipher, and the deed is done. Go left, down the Elevator, and kill the foe on the other side. Note where you are, since you'll need to return to this spot. Go left, up the slopes, onto the platform, and head right. Go up the Elevator at the end of the platform, head left, pass over all the Elevators, then go through the door and fight Badger. Do this by jumping; he'll jump with you, but you'll come down first. When you do, slip under him and attack his back when he lands. A few such attacks and he's dead meat. Go left and destroy the system here. Head right, back over the rows of Elevators, and return to the spot you noted above. There, go left, down the first Elevator, and into the room on the right. Go down the Elevator, head left, read the message, continue left, head down the elevator . . . and prepare for a series of encounters consisting of fight, Elevator, fight, Elevator, and so on . . . until you face the chief baddie!

Par: A good player should be able to get as far as the Red Dragon headquarters in time. Again, the skills you'll use in each country are more or less the same; if you can do one, you can do them all.

Training Tips: Use the last code to go to the Red Dragon headquarters. Try fighting your way through with just your basic weaponry—a character builder if ever there was one!

Rating: Having to discover clues and hop back and forth between countries makes this game interesting. The only real drawback is that very few of the enemies put up much of a fight. The animation and scenery are exceptional.

    Challenge: B
    Graphics: A
    Sound Effects: B

CHAPTER TWENTY-ONE

SUPER DODGE BALL

Type: International sports competition. .

Manufacturer: CSG Imagesoft Inc., under license from Nintendo.

Objective: Taking opposite sides of the court, one team must try to eliminate the other by beaning players with a basketball-sized Ball. There's also a Bean Ball game, which is just a lot of undisciplined fun!

Layout: The screen has a small degree of horizontal scroll as the Ball is tossed from side to side. There are eight teams playing against you. Each has appropriate scenery; the only aberrations in the playing field are a slightly slippery court in Iceland and a very sluggish dirt court in Kenya.

Hero: Each of the eight teams' players has individual strengths and weaknesses. All players can walk, run, pass, throw, jump, duck, or catch. Players also have super-throw specialties, which are discussed below. Many players will surprise you, however, and come up with an occasional super-throw you didn't know they had in them! These are beyond your control to predict. You can select three of six available players to man the Inner Court, and you can control the players in the Outer Court, though these are low-powered. You can only move one player at a time.

Enemies: Same as the heroes. In order of appearance when you fight the computer (and in order of difficulty), the teams are: Pro All-Stars, England, India, Iceland, China, Kenya, Japan, USSR. Be aware that the players in the Outer Court, while not nearly as effective as the players in the Inner Court, can still inflict damage (usually two points) when they hit you.

Menu: Two players can bop each other, or one player can battle the computer.

Scoring: There are no points. Players lose energy depending upon the strength of the hit they take; there is no way to reclaim lost energy. How many points you lose depends upon who hits you and how close you are to the impact (a player taking a hit at center court from an opponent at center court is going to suffer more than someone in the backcourt). Winners advance to match-ups with successively more difficult teams. A note about the confusing team charts in the back of the instruction booklet. It says, for example, that Helgi of the

Iceland team has 64 points of Damage Capacity . . . yet on the screen it shows only 16 bars. What you must do is multiply the number of bars on the TV screen by four, so it'll match the number in the book. Notice that when each player is hit, a number appears above his head. This shows the amount of damage that was done. Since the bars on top of the screen disappear only in increments of four, this may be misleading. For example, if a character starts 20 points strong (meaning that there are five bars), and 15 damage points are inflicted, only three bars will disappear. Two will be left on the screen, and it'll look like the character can still take eight damage points. Not so! It'll only take five damage points to eliminate him.

Beginner's Strategy: If you're playing the computer, the best American team you can field consists of Sam, Bill, and Steve. Sam can throw a Blaster (see instructions for definitions of this and all special throws), and is also very strong against Rajiv of the team from India. Bill can use both the Spear and the Lightning (extremely valuable against China; he can knock up to 24 points from a man!), while Steve almost always relies on the Spear . . . though he'll surprise you sometimes and throw a Breaker. As for the other Americans, they're good too: John throws a Sidewinder, and when jumping, usually lets go with a Psycho; Mike is almost exclusively

Sidewinder; Randy usually flings a Stinger (which looks like a coin flipped horizontally).

A few general tips. When an opponent throws a jump shot, the ball will often leave the top of the screen. Keep your eye on the small shadow it casts so you'll know where it's coming down.

Keep your eye on your enemy's lineup. See who's got the ball. If it's a powerful thrower, make sure you switch control to your best catcher. (It's a judgment call as to whether you should risk your best catcher if he's already low on energy; most players opt to take the chance, rather than take damage on a bad catcher who's otherwise in good shape.)

In the early going protect your strongest players: you'll need them at full-capacity for the tougher foes later on. For example, have someone else do the catching for Sam—though it's okay to pass the ball for him to shoot.

Another thing to watch out for is the enemy pass. Your opponent's Inner Court players will frequently throw the ball to an Outer Court player, who will immediately spike it down the throat of the athlete nearest him. When you see the pass, jump up and intercept it. You may suffer a bit of damage getting in the way, but it's less than you'll endure if the other player catches it and bounces it off your skull.

Finally, if one of your players is hit, get someone else over quickly to recover the ball. If not, one of your adversary's Outer Court players may get the ball and deliver a second blow before your man can get up. By the same token, if one of your opponents gets decked, make sure you get your Outer Court player over to recover the ball and hit him fast!

Advanced Strategy: When you become adept at controlling the ball, one of the most satisfying shots you can make is the jump shot that carries you well over the center-court line. You can't touch down with the ball in your hand—but you can leap well into your opponent's side and release it while you're still in the air. You will wreak a lot more damage hitting them so close. (Just make sure you turn tail and run back to your side before they catch the ball and hit you equally as close!)

One really neat strategy is trapping the other team's player at the center-court line. If they run up to hit you, and you catch it, don't bother running the ball to the backcourt then running it in again. Simply pass it back and clobber your opponent before he has a chance to beat it too far!

Par: An average player battling the computer will get as far as a close match with Kenya, which is the first of the really difficult teams.

Training Tips: Use the Bean Ball mode to master ball control and player movement. There are no rules or restrictions, which is terrific for honing your skills: you just get the ball and blitz each other!

Rating: This cartridge is different from anything else that's out there, and is a great solo or party game. There are three difficulty levels, which makes it perfect for all age and experience groups.

Challenge: A

Graphics: B (There's occasional image breakup, which can be distracting during a heated match; however, the characterization and animation are nifty when players are clobbered—they go flying when hit, and weep when they lose—and the scenery is attractive.)

Sound Effects: A (Excellent music, which evokes each nation.)

CHAPTER TWENTY-TWO

SUPER SPRINT
(A TENGEN GAME)

Type: Auto racing game.

Manufacturer: Tengen. Not designed, manufactured, sponsored or endorsed by Nintendo.®

Objective: It's the Grand Prix time, and your goal is to complete five laps first against a crowded field, while avoiding the various obstacles thrown in your way.

Layout: The view is from above, as you race through seven different tracks. With track number 8, these repeat; beginning with number 14 they repeat with the addition of three poles that pop up and block the road at various points. The tracks are roughly shaped as follows:

1. *N shape*
2. *Uppercase B shape*
3. *Elongated N shape*
4. *& and D shape left and right, respectively*

5. *S and backward S shape side by side*
6. *Flat C atop a figure 8*
7. *Overlapping squares*

The poles appear in these positions (always the same), and rise and fall (at which point they're harmless) with a regular cadence:

14. *Three in a row on the right*
15. *Three diagonally, in the center*
16. *Two top right, one middle left*
17. *Three at the shortcut on the top*
18. *Two left, one right*
19. *Three scattered*
20. *Three in the tough left loop*

Hero: Despite the overhead view, you steer your car from the point of view of the driver's seat. This takes some getting used to. There are Wrenches scattered on the tracks; you can customize your car each time you obtain a pair of these. You only get to do so, however, if you win the race. You can only use each of the four customizing options up to six times. These choices are described in the booklet. Although the Wrenches appear in random spots on each track, they almost always appear when the car in the lead completes its first and fourth laps. You can advance to each new track only by winning the one you're on. Smack-ups result in a momentary disabling of the cars.

Enemies: Among the enemy cars, white is always

the fastest and toughest. The longer play goes on, the faster *all* the opposing cars become. When they pick up Wrenches, nothing happens—except that you're deprived of the prize! Inexplicably, enemy cars sometimes skip loops as they race through the course. If they (or you, for that matter) do so, or take loops in the wrong direction, nothing you do thereafter counts. So, keep an eye on opponents who do this. They're no longer a threat. In addition to the other cars, there are six impediments from Mud Puddles to Tornadoes, which are discussed in the booklet and also below. You don't lose points for hitting any of these . . . just time.

Menu: Two players can race against each other, with computer-controlled cars adding to the fun, or one player can battle the field of computer-run vehicles. In a two-player mode, both players advance to the next track if one of them wins. If one player is way behind with no chance of winning, it may be in everyone's best interests to smash into whatever car is hot on the other player's fender.

Scoring: You earn points as you pass checkpoints on each track or by running over Red Flags which appear at random. See instructions for breakdown. Wrenches (see *Hero)* also boost your score.

Beginner's Strategy: In general, it's nonsporting but important to cut off either your opponent's car or the white car. Doing this at the starting line can be especially beneficial, since you'll take the lead and get first crack at the Wrench. Upon obtaining Wrenches, always acquire power-ups in this order: Super Traction, Higher Top Speed, Turbo Accelerator, and Increase Score. Most players prefer to boost Traction to the full six levels before going to another option, especially when playing only the computer; you won't need speed as much as a good grip on the road in the early going.

A few tips on the courses. Number 3 is the best for cutting off opponents because of the many turns. Take these in a diagonal movement, cutting across the loop rather than following its turn. You'll not only cut off adversaries, you'll save time. Number 4 has a shortcut: a vertical passage where the fence is broken in the center. Cut across the grass here to save time. On number 5 note that there's also a break in two fences on top; just treat the top part of the screen as if it were a straightaway.

Two final tips on dealing with adversity. If you get caught in a Tornado, turn your car in the same direction you're spinning. That will restore control quickly. And if you go nose first into a wall, immediately release the accelerator button, turn in the direction you want to go, and rev up. If you try to feed the car gas to get out of the jam, all you'll do is send yourself back into the wall or into the spin. Do this, too, when you crash beneath an underpass. You won't be able to see which way you're pointing, so just let up on the gas, point *some* way, and then hit the pedal to nudge the car back into view. Aim and take off!

Advanced Strategy: The most important skill to master in the later levels is the "comet" maneuver to get you through the loops. This works especially well in the fourth track, top-left loop, and in all the loops of number 5. You shoot through them with your front end constantly facing the triangle in the center of the loop. You can perform this maneuver at top speed (something you can't do while steering) by moving the joystick or controller just before you enter the loop, so that you literally enter it sideways. You'll not only cut down on time by entering it at high speed, but you'll be facing the exit when you complete the turn. When you become skillful, you can also use the "carom" maneuver to your advantage, actually hitting the side of the course so you can make turns without slowing down. This works like a charm on the lower straightaway of the second course. Coming out of the curve on the bottom left, you cut diagonally across the straightaway along the bottom, hit the corner on the bottom right side, and shoot upward.

Par: You should be earning 10,000 points per winning lap.

Training Tips: Play the computer, and give the other cars a head start. It'll steel your nerves and reflexes by forcing you to compete at top speed.

Rating: A good game for one player, but lots of fun for two. The only drawback is the lack of variety in the courses. The animation of the cars is good.

    Challenge: B
    Graphics: B
    Sound Effects: B

CHAPTER TWENTY-THREE

THUNDERCADE

Type: Military shoot-'em-up.

Manufacturer: American Sammy, under license from Nintendo.

Objective: The terrorist group AATOM (Atomic Age Terrorist Organization of Miracali) has built a nuclear power plant that endangers the world. The endangered nations of the planet put together a crack team of antiterrorists, of which you're the leader. Your mission: penetrate AATOM lines and destroy the facility.

Layout: The screen scrolls vertically, and the view is from overhead. There are four zones in all.

Hero: Riding your Combat Cycle, you can jump obstacles, shoot at the enemy, and also acquire bonus items. The most important of these are Sidecars, each of which boosts your firepower; these are described in the instruction booklet. The Vulcan is the most important of these, and you should go for one at all costs. (Be careful not to run over a Sidecar after you've acquired Vulcan; the new one will supplant the old one.) You can carry up to two Sidecars; one is lost each time you're shot. The hero has the ability to summon air cover, a Bomb strike that will destroy everything to the Cycle's left and right . . . but only in the immediate vicinity. You can call the Bombers three times; more, if you've picked up bonus Bombs. Upon completing certain portions of the mission, you are spirited to a bonus round, in which an airplane drops Vulcans, 1-Ups, and other necessary items. You only get to keep the ones you catch.

Enemies: These range from Soldiers to Tanks to Missiles to Gunships, all of which are illustrated in the instructions. There are also nonpartisan Obstacles, some of which can be destroyed for points (and conceal bonus weapons), some of which can't and must be jumped. Incidentally, if you collide with an enemy Tank, don't sweat it. You'll pass right through it, as long as the Tank isn't firing.

Menu: One player can play alone, or two can enjoy the game at the same time. Just be careful: while one player can't accidentally shoot the other in a two-player mode, one player can accidentally *bump* the other into enemy fire. It's a quick way to make an enemy . . . for real!

Scoring: You earn points for killing enemy soldiers and vehicles; these are described in the instructions. You also get points for everything the Bombers destroy.

Beginner's Strategy: Overall, always try to use buildings and trees for shelter. Even though you're on the side of these objects, they can also protect you from Helicopters, Jets, Missiles, and other airborne foes. Just remember that just as Bullets can't hit you, your fire can't reach the enemy.

Here's a stage-by-stage guide to beating the game.

City: The first Sidecar is on the right; make sure you attach it to your left side, since most of the early foes will be coming from there. You'll find your first Vulcan in the building to the right shortly after the stationary Truck in the center of the screen. When the Helicopters arrive, just blast them with Vulcan; if you're anxious about the number of enemies here, call for the first Bomber attack. Definitely send for the Bombers if you've lost Vulcan; you'll have a tough time shooting down the choppers otherwise. If you've lost all your Sidecars, you'll find one by shooting the Tree in the bottom corner of the first Park on your left. When you reach the Submarine, the screen will stop scrolling. Go to the lower left corner and nudge the controller slightly so that you're just in from the left side of the screen; shoot the personnel coming in from the left. The Sub's fire won't reach you there.

When the screen begins to scroll again, head to the road at the top of the screen. When a rooftop appears on the left side of the screen, you can snuggle yourself between it and the buildings to its right; ride that alley for protection, if you need a break. A second Vulcan is hidden just ahead, in the second building on the right once the rooftop appears; uncover it with an air strike or run over and shoot the building, but make sure you get it. The road will fork in just a moment, and traffic will be really heavy. Stay on the right side; there are fewer enemies there. A narrow roadway will pass between two bodies of water, after which you'll face the Gunship. Call for a Bomber attack; two, if you have any left over. The Gunship has five guns pointed at you from the top of the screen, and the Bomber will take out most of these. To destroy the guns that remain (or to take them all out in case you were out of Bombers), go to one of the two far sides and position yourself slightly in from that side. There are "sweet spots" where the guns can't hit you. As the Gunship shifts from side to side, however, *you* can shoot *it*. You'll know you've hit a gun when sparks fly. Hold your ground and keep firing until the gun is destroyed, then slide over and shoot the next.

Base: Head up the center and get a 1-Up from the building on the right. If you need a Sidecar, there's one on the left after the first Turrets (uncover it with an air strike . . . which is also useful in getting rid of the Turrets). Attach the Sidecar to your left side.

There's nothing too dangerous here until you come to the stepped plateaus with Turrets on either side. Ride up the center and *keep on jumping* to avoid their fire. Jets will strafe you after you clear these; shoot them down or dodge them, but get to the right, so you can be on the runway when it shows up. There will be a seemingly endless stream of Tanks to the left, with which you'll want to avoid colliding. Shoot them with your left-facing Sidecar. After you've passed the runway, stay on the right and jump on top of the bunkers as long as you can. There's a 1-Up in the Bunker on the left in the ammunition area (before the Missiles); there's another 1-Up in the last Missile. Make sure you shoot and destroy both to acquire these. You'll need all the extra lives you can get! After you pass through the narrow green strip of grass, you'll face another Gunship. Destroy this one as before, then go to the Bonus round.

Advanced Strategy: Continuing the stage-by-stage guide:

Wood Lands: Obtain a bomb from the first Bunker on the right. When you reach the bridge, summon your Bomber: it's a killer! In the woods use the trees for shelter as you fire. There's a Vulcan in the trees to the right after the first set of Turrets; you'll find a 1-Up in the trees just beyond it, to the left. Use your Vulcan power to shoot the choppers, then blast the new set of Turrets; after you clear them, there's a 1-Up in the first Bunker to the right.

After this, the lineup of Turrets changes; they're situated in a row that stretches across the screen. You'll have to blast them rather than skirt their fire. The field afterward will be crawling with Tanks, so be prepared to summon your Bomber. There's another field with a four-Turret lineup ahead, and another field after that; surprisingly, there's no big finish to this stage. Go to the bonus stage.

Fortress: This one's murder. After you fight an assault from Soldiers and Tanks, there are three Turrets with nothing inside. Passing these, you'll be in an open area with nowhere to hide; you've got to shoot everything. Worse, Missiles come flying in with alarming frequency and speed. These will have to be ducked or shot with Vulcan; not much else works against them. When you reach the Missile launchers, just shoot them to destroy them; they're the easiest foe on this level. Deal with your next foe, the Submarine, as you did before; another Submarine follows, after which you'll find yourself on a blue field heavily populated with Soldiers and Bunkers. There's a 1-Up in the second Bunker. Fighting your way to the concrete field, you'll find a 105mm Cannon Sidecar. It's the next best thing to a Vulcan you can have! Watch for the Hangars on the right and top, which will send a steady stream of Tanks in your direction. These are followed by Bunkers on the left, then right, and Barracks (which send out Soldiers) straight ahead. The next section of Fortress presents a Barracks on the right, a

Tank Hangar on the left, and a Barracks above. You'd be wise to call in a Bomber at this point. Clearing this area, you'll come to a solid wall up ahead; shoot down the doors (or let your Bomber do it) and pass through—there's a Sidecar in the doors, if you need it. The final impediment between you and your target is an unbelievable nest of Tanks. These rise from sliding doors in the pavement in incredible numbers, all of them spitting motor-cycle-seeking Missiles at a super-rapid-fire pace. Though you'll want to have Bombers left over for your nuclear target at the end, if you don't call them now, you won't *reach* the end. The power plant is anticlimactic after this barrage of Tanks.

Par: A good player will earn 45,000 points per level. You should have to take no more than 500 shots to complete a game; 40 percent is a good hit ratio.

Training Tips: Play the game without using Bomber cover. Your motorcycling skills will improve fast . . . or you'll have a super-short mission!

Rating: The different kinds of Sidecars, and the constant flood of foes, makes for a doozy of a ride!
> *Challenge:* B+
> *Graphics:* C (The Bombers are the only really neat visual; the animation is mediocre.)
> *Sound Effects:* B

CHAPTER TWENTY-FOUR

XENOPHOBE

Type: Science fiction shoot-'em-up.

Manufacturer: Sunsoft, under license from Nintendo.

Objective: A xenophobe is someone who fears aliens. In this game they have a darn good reason: the alien Xenos are invading space bases and ready to kill anyone who gets in their way.

Layout: The screen scrolls horizontally. There are eight different space bases, with eight floors in each—and very little variety between them, we might add!

Hero: You can choose to be one of three Exterminators: Mr. Fogg, Dr. Kwack, or Dr. Zoriaz. Your selection is purely aesthetic and has no strategic value. In the beginning your Xeno-hunter has a weak gun and the ability to squat, crawl, or jump. By killing Xenos he acquires more powerful weapons as well as

JEFF ROVIN

Medicine and other items outlined in the booklet. The items given by monsters, and the monsters who give them, are entirely random. Regardless, they stay on the screen for ten seconds before vanishing.

Enemies: There are five different kinds of Xenos, which are described in the instructions and below. These include the lovely Snotterpillar, which spits goo at you; try and guess what kind of goo! With the exception of Spiderions and Laser Balls, the monsters materialize out of thin air, anywhere, any time.

Menu: One player can fight aliens alone, or two can fight side by side.

Scoring: The player gets weapons as well as points for killing Xenos. The points range from 100 for Critters to 500 for Spiderions; you also earn points for picking up weapons or items. At the same time, hits from the monsters cost the player Health Damage proportionate to their point value. These are all detailed in the instructions.

Beginner's Strategy: A few basic tips to remember. First, if you acquire a more sophisticated weapon, you can't take it with you to another floor. Second, try to keep your power no lower than the 1000 mark, and definitely not below the 500 level. All it takes is a tenacious Snotterpillar to run you down to zero from there. If you need energy, stop at a room where there are no Laser Balls (they're toughest to kill) or Elevators (Snotterpillars have a way of materializing inside, where they're really tough to see). Preferably, go to one where there are Spiderions. Kill them, collect whatever they drop, leave the room, turn and reenter, and repeat. Spiderions won't necessarily drop the Medicine you need every time, but you should get some often enough.

The reason you should stick with the Spiderions is that they tend to be on the sides of the room. If you stand right inside their doorway, beside them, their bombs rarely touch you. Or if they're on the other side of the room, while their bombs can't reach you, your Bullets can reach them (unless you have one of the advanced weapons, which are more powerful but have a shorter range). The caveat here is that if you kill a Spiderion on the far side of the room, and a monster materializes between you and whatever item the dead Spiderion dropped, you may not get to the goody before it vaporizes. It's best to get in all but the last shot or two, then move close to the Spiderion and finish it off.

It's also wise to retreat to a doorway whenever you have to fight a Snotterpillar. If you crouch there and fail to get off enough rounds to kill it, the alien usually leaps over you—not hurting you, and also not returning. In a closed room the creature will simply bounce off the shut door, double back, and attack again. Also, in a doorway, if it does try to maul you, you can always duck out; creatures don't follow you from room to room. And, crouching, you're less likely to be hit by one of its energy-sapping slimeballs.

A word about leaving rooms and reentering. If you killed a Laser Ball, then leave a room and come back, it will be there again—but not where you killed it. It'll be exactly where it was when you first entered the room. Be aware of where it was, and enter firing!

Also, when you come to Laser Barriers, you can leave and forget about them . . . or you can walk through them. It'll take a few tries and cost you a lot of energy, but it's usually worth it. Incidentally, try not to kill monsters that materialize on the other side of the Barrier. Wait until they charge through, or you may not be able to get to whatever item they leave behind.

Advanced Strategy: In order to rack up points, it's a good idea to move through each room at a crawl instead of walking. You move more slowly, but the bulk of the monsters are most vulnerable at that height level.

For the most part, whenever you enter a new floor, there's time to get the lay of the land before you have to start shooting. The notable exceptions are places like 1/3, where you enter and find yourself in a tight space between two Spiderions. Quickly step to one side, turn, and blast them. Another tip about Spiderions is this: if you've just started an attack on one and a Snotterpillar materializes, don't leave the room; you'll only have to start the Spiderion attack from scratch, and chances are good a Snotterpillar will come again anyway. Use the leap-the-Snotterpillar technique described in *Training Tips* to deal with the situation.

Par: Scores change as you climb to different floors, since there are more monsters and more items to grab. The cumulative progression of a good player is roughly this: 1/1: 25,000 points. 1/2: 65,000. 1/3: 120,000. 1/4: 200,000. The scores increase by approximately 100,000 points each floor thereafter.

Training Tips: Most players tend to rely too much on their shooting ability. Practice your jumping; this can be especially useful against Snotterpillars. You can get in some shots before they move, jump when they charge, turn, fire, and repeat if necessary.

Rating: For all the potential in the game, it's surprisingly tame. There's plenty of time to act; you rarely face any real pressure. However, a tip of the space helmet to the people who designed the instruction booklet. There's simulated slime on all the pages, giving the manual an air of verisimilitude.

Challenge: C+

Graphics: C+ (a little too cartoony)

Sound Effects: D (not many effects at all!)

NINTEN-DO'S AND DON'TS— INCLUDING DETAILED NEW STRATEGIES FOR SUPER MARIO BROS. 2 AND TEENAGE MUTANT NINJA TURTLES!

As in the previous books, here's a generous helping of tips for games other than those covered up front.

First, and most important, here's more on everyone's favorite fantasy game, *Super Mario Bros. 2*.

Topping the list are some Warp locations, which you will definitely want to try.

In World 3/1, take a trip down the Waterfall. Go into the room at the bottom and claim the Potion buried beneath the Grass (third clump from the left). Climb into the Jar there and you'll be spirited ahead to 5/1.

You can perform this next maneuver best if you're high-jumping Luigi. (We gave this a quick write-up in our previous coverage of the game; here are more details.) On level 4/2 you'll encounter a Jar on an island after the last and largest Whale of the second pod of Whales. You'll have earned Potion, and you must carry it *beyond* the Jar, to the tail of the next Whale to the right. Turn left, return to the island, and put the Potion on top. When you're in subspace, enter the Jar and you'll skip World 5, landing in 6/1. (And while we're on the subject, here's a correction . . . and an apology! When we were preparing our original write-up, some Nintendummy thought "dark Whales" was a mistake and changed it to "dark stone walls"! Sorry about that. Hopefully, you knew what we meant.)

Assuming you went ahead and played World 5, here's how you can skip World 6 and go right to 7/1; again, you need to be Luigi to make this work. After you climb the Ladder and get Potion, return to the left and take a super-jump so you're near the top of the Jar. Toss the Potion here, enter the Jar when you're in subspace, and hold onto your trousers as you're whisked ahead! A few less exiting Warps are mentioned below.

So much for short-cuts. In the first, updated volume of *How to Win at Nintendo Games,* we only went into detail through the end of the third World. Here's a complete rundown of additional levels. But first—a few things we neglected to mention last time.

1. *Toad picks things up faster than the other characters.*
2. *The Princess levitates for 3 seconds.*
3. *We forgot to mention Mouser in the* Enemies *section. (He paid us a visit to make sure it didn't happen again. Happy, creep?)*
4. *On page 198, where we talk about Phanto pursuing you: if you're Luigi, you can forgo the Door altogether, if you want to. When you reach the monster jumping up and down beside the wall, pick the creature up, move it closer to the mountain, and jump onto its back. When it rises, use your super-jump to leap to the top of the mountain.*

Okay. Onward to World 4.

To begin with, it's slippery, so proceed with caution. When you've crossed the third platform on top, jump down: on the far end of the bottom platform is Potion, just beneath the end of the platform above it. After you go down the ice steps a little farther on, leap across to the next island, where you'll find more Potion on the left edge of the top ledge. Go to the right ledge and fall off. There's a Rocket tucked in the left corner of the platform on the bottom.

You'd be wise to use Luigi for the next part, since his jumping power will prove mighty useful. There's Grass on the third ledge in, on the bottom. When you reach the second ledge, jump up to the top ledge. Upon reaching the end, run off the edge, land on the bottom ledge to the right, skid (that's right, *skid*) right across it and grab the Grass as you're sliding. Jump up through the top ledge, where no one will attack you. Cross over to the next ledge, use the Potion near the Grass, and enter subspace. Nothing else terribly extraordinary happens on this level. When you reach the end (the layout is quite similar to where you found the last Rocket), jump down as you did before. There's no Rocket here—just Grass. However, when you pull it out, the Rocket will appear.

Your biggest challenge in the next part will be the threat of the Autobomb, which is a Mario-Brothers-seeking missile which spits fire to boot. What to do? Destroy the Shyguy on top and take its place on the bomb! Not only will this protect you, but you'll be able to hitch a ride over some lethal spikes.

In short order you'll find yourself at 4/2. We've already told you about the Warp; here's the rest of the information you'll need to get through.

Climb the Vine and head right. Toward the end of the long ledge you'll be pestered by Flurries. Don't ignore them: if you don't kill them, they'll stay on your tail. The next crucial event in your journey is when you emerge from the door atop the cloud. Go to the right until you get to the three, fat islands. Go to the top of the largest one (on the right). Pick the Grass, get the Potion, throw it next to you, on the left, and get the Coins. Go left, to the door where you were at the beginning, and exit. (Reenter and repeat, if you want.) Another subspace can be accessed by going left, getting the Potion from the back of the Whale, and using it to create a new subspace where you obtain Mushrooms. (Can you cause both subspaces to appear? Try it and see!)

Continue to the right, over the Whales. The ninth Whale in has a powerful Waterspout which you can ride to an upper ledge; it's rich in Cherries, and worth the risk (the risk being if you hit any part of the Waterspout other than the top, you'll be hurt). The Rocket out of here is on the big island past the tenth Whale.

The next level pits you against another Shyguy/Autobomb combination, and the aforementioned ride across the spikes. You've got to get the Cherries on the ceiling here, as they're the only way to summon Starman, who is the only one that can help you defeat Porcupo at the end of the spikes. Otherwise, there's nothing to worry about here. Upon entering a door to the right, you'll find yourself in a dark room . . . the lair of Birdo. Since the fiend will be tossing Eggs, and the floor is tough to stand on, you'd be wise to get on the ledge beneath Birdo's, jump up, catch an Egg when thrown (don't be impulsive and try to catch any fireballs, which this

Birdo also disgorges!), and toss it back at the monster.

Now you're at 4/3. Go right, get the Potion from atop the building, head left, and open a subspace door on the top of the leftmost pole. Get the Mushroom from the top of the central pole, leave subspace, head right, and you'll immediately confront another Birdo—which is fine, since you'll have to use the monster's Egg to ride right, over the water, to get to the door of the first tower—past the steps and on the right side of the ledge beyond them. (Don't try to leap or hover over the water between the two towers; none of the characters can make it.) Start making your way to the top of the tower, taking care to go to the right when you encounter the deadly floor of Icicles on the left. Reaching the top (after carefully dodging Flurries on the icy ledges), you go out the door, head right, and pluck the Grasses on the bridge between this tower and the one to the right. Use the Clouds on the left to ascend to the top of that tower, open a subspace door, and get yourself a Mushroom.

Enter the second tower. Ride Shyguy over the Icicles, then drop down the long vertical passageway in the middle. There's a door on the ledge below; enter, get the key (kill Flurries with it, if you're attacked), and go to the door at the bottom of the tower. Enter, and if you find yourself back at the beginning of the level, head to the far right, to the door beyond the two towers (the one you haven't yet entered). Hurry to the right, to the Mask, and enter the realm of Fryguy. In the dead center of the screen are two

Mushrooms. Pick up the Mushroom on the left, moving back quickly so you don't fall through. Drop it on Fryguy when the hothead passes underneath. Repeat this procedure using the Mushroom on the right, then go down to the Mushrooms on the bottom and pelt the villain; three direct hits and he'll fall apart into four mini-Fryguys. Each of these will attack, but they're easier to block and kill than their progenitor.

Easy as ABC, right?

Before we go on to the rest of the worlds, here's a way to fill your piggybank to overflowing if you have some extra lives to spare. In 5/1 you'll come across five Grasses on a cliff. Use Potion here, go to subspace, gather the Grass . . . and jump off the cliff. That's right: swan dive to oblivion. You'll materialize back at the beginning of 5/1. Do this again and again, gathering coins until you don't want to give up any more lives.

If you've gotten this far, congrats! Here are some Mar(io)velous tips for the remaining levels of the game.

5/1: Use Trouters and Logs to cross the Waterfalls. If you have Luigi, then getting across with a jump or two will be easy. If you're not Luigi, it will be necessary to leap from Trouter-head to Trouter-head up to three times to get across. It's a tricky maneuver, but one which must be mastered to get to the other side. At the end of the level, Birdo spits flame, and can only be defeated by the Mushroom Block on the other side of the fiend. Jump to it with care!

5/2: Subspace is a little different than you're used to. You won't find any Potion in the Grasses. You'll have to enter the Jar, toss a Bomb, and open up a room beneath you. The Potion is in there. Get it and use it as usual. When you reach the Vines, stay on the one on the right. A Hoopster haunts the left one! Upon reaching the Bridge, take the POW and let yourself drop through the opening. As you drop, maneuver to avoid the Icicles (aka Thorns). When you finally see the water coming up at you, jockey Mario to the right so he lands on the shore.

5/3: This area opens with a Warp Zone, as described above. If you'd rather slug it out here instead of chickening out and blasting off to World 7, beware the Bob-Omb-dropping Albatoss (sic) in the next subspace (atop the first grassy plateau). After you climb down the ladder, avoid (repeat: AVOID) the Mushroom Block to the right. It'll open a Pandora's Box of Bob-Ombs. The level's third subspace is found after you head left and reach the ledge before the looming red wall. Just wait there until Bob-Ombs fall: You'll need them to blow up the vertical barrier beneath your feet, which prevents you from reaching the Potion-Grasses. When you finally reach the vertical chamber, the gravest foe you'll face are the Pansers. Fortunately, you can always leave the screen on one side and re-enter on the other to escape. Upon confronting the boss, Clawgrip, duck the Rocks it spits, then pick the boulders up and hurl 'em right back.

6/1: Subspace the first is located at the Jar. Enter it, pull out the Grass, and fling the potion onto the Bones. A Mushroom will appear: Nab it at once, or it'll be swallowed up as quickly as it appeared. The biggest puzzler on this level is the Jar room. There're twenty-one of them, a real time-waster to search. So: go to the third Jar from the right for a 1-Up, and the fifth Jar from the right for the Key you need.

6/2: Albatosses are your enemies, of course, but you're going to have to ride them, piggy-back, to get across the chasms in the early going. Subspace is located at the third and fourth columns shortly after the beginning of the level. Leave your Albatoss taxi, get off on the column with the Grasses, and grab the one on the left. In order to exit subspace, you'll have to hitch a lift on a leftward-flying Albatoss, which will carry you back to the beginning of the level. The boss of 6/2 is none other than one more fire-spitting Birdo. Beat him by dropping a pair of Mushroom Blocks from the ledge overhead, and a third from the left side.

6/3: In the desert, go left, and you'll warp to 6/4. Go right for adventure. But do *something:* you're standing on quicksand. Pull up the Grass to the right of the Ladder, hop to the second Bone (remember, you'll sink if you stand still), and enter subspace here. Continuing to the right, you'll come to a stone abode. Inside, climb the first Ladder and just hang on it to avoid the Bob-Ombs. Then continue right, gathering Cherries. Don't destroy the wall after the third Sand Pit; you'll be overwhelmed by Ninjis. Blast the wall below, get the Starman, and skedaddle. To get to the next subspace, Cherry-bomb all the bricks you can, then go right, to the Ladder, descend, blast the wall to the left, climb back up the Ladder, Potion in hand, and drop through the opening. You'll do some Vine-climbing next, which will require some Donkey Kong-like horizontal shifting from Vine-to-Vine. When you meet Birdo, beat the birdie with its own Eggs, then get set for Tryclyde. Stack the Mushroom Blocks three high to get above the monster's fiery breath, then crown it with the remaining Blocks.

7/1: Climb, ride an Albatoss to the left, pull the Grass, ride the Rocket, and gird your loins for what lies ahead. Or, climb and hike to the right—quickly when you're between the columns, or your enemies will blast the bridge from 'neath your feet! When you reach the Column with the Grass, pull it out, retrace your steps to the left, and drop the Potion on the roof of the House. Welcome to subspace! When you reach the second House, enter, go to the fifth clump of Grass from the left, and use it to access subspace. When you emerge, hop onto an Albatoss heading left and continue as described at the beginning of this section. When you reach the vertical Cloud section, you're going to run into trouble about midway up: In order to span the gap between the last section of Clouds, you'll have to build a platform of Mushroom Blocks.

7/2: You begin the homestretch, the assault on Wart's Castle, with a stroll across the moving floors. Pretty pedestrian stuff. When you come to the Chain, you can descend, or you can ignore it and continue to the right. Going down enables you to avoid a small chunk of this realm by entering the door at the bottom. If you take this route, pick Cherries and call on a Starman. Head right and enter the first door you encounter. This leads you to a secret room with Potion; use it to enter subspace, and fill your life meter as much as possible. Leave, and continue to the right, entering the next door you find.

Climb the Chain through the vertical chamber, pass through the horizontal room, ascend the next vertical passageway which is full of moving floors (not so much fun as the first room of sliding floors), head left when you can, leaping Birdo, climb again, and note where you are (we'll dub this point "R"). Go right, ignoring the doors, for now. Climb down the Chain at the far right, get the Key, and retrace your steps to the door with the Keyhole. Enter and face Wart.

Now . . . remember, way back when, when you could have gone down or to the right? If you went right, you made the better choice. (Why didn't we tell you? Birdo held an Egg to our heads.) Had you taken this route, you'd have had to make your way through just one horizontal chamber and a pair of vertical passages (entering the door midway up the first to access the second, then coming down to get into a secret room). At the top of the vertical stone passageway, there's a door which would have taken you right to point "R". (Why "R"? It stands for, "Rats! I should've gone this way!")

No matter for regrets, though: It's time for a

Warty Party. Though he'll be expectorating disgusting things at you, concentrate on getting the Vegetables which come popping from the Dream Machine. Hitting him with this is the only way to slay the frog-like lunatic. Be careful, though: You can only hurt him by throwing the Veggies into his mouth when it's open.

And there you have it! The complete *Super Mario Bros. 2!*

Before turning to some important new strategies on *Teenage Mutant Ninja Turtles,* here's a rundown of tips for other new and classic Nintendo games—some of which we covered in the previous books, some new to our lineup.

Golgo 13: When you're in enemy strongholds, there's a way to tap your Life Meter should you find yourself in need of the bullets. Simply push Select and you'll be able to make the swap.

Rambo: Many players find the Flying Fortress quite intimidating and would prefer to avoid it altogether. Here's how you can do just that. When Rambo arrives at the cell of the last POW, have him enter, but take care not to knock down the top block of the cell wall. Leave the cell, do an about-face, and reenter, with the prisoner tagging behind. Go to the right wall, push the A button over and over while simultaneously pushing the joystick left, then right. Rambo will begin burrowing up through top of the cell using his head. Eventually the warrior will reach his chopper.

Jackal: If you're playing a two-player game and one player dies for the last time, don't let that person perish in vain! As she or he is in the act of dying, push your A and B buttons at the same time. If your timing is exact (which requires some luck), your companion will receive over 100 extra lives! A more modest way of returning from the dead is this—assuming the other player has a spare Jeep. After losing your own last life, push the A and B buttons simultaneously. Your partner will lose a Jeep, but you'll return to active duty!

Sky Kid: A pretty mediocre cartridge, this, but some of you may be picking it up as a discount item, so: if you want to continue the game, push the second controller down and left and, while holding it there, press Start on the first controller.

Spy Hunter: You can obtain ten extra cars by doing the following. When the title screen comes on, push the joystick to the right and hold it there while pushing Start and Select at the same time. Your ten cars will be added when the timer runs out. Also, if you want to start the game with all your weapons, wait until the title screen comes on, then press A, B, and Select at the same time.

Metal Gear: In case you haven't figured this out by now, we thought we'd mention it: you can't blow up the Super Computer unless you've first saved Dr. Petrovich's daughter. Accomplishing that, you should be able to destroy the unit with around a dozen charges. Having said that, if you want to avoid the Super Computer altogether, here's what you do. Upon entering the room and facing Solid Snake, press the joystick to the right. You'll be sent right to Outer Heaven's room.

Kid Icarus: Two codes that will bring you to the last level of play are: DANGER !!!!!! TERROR HORROR, while 8uuuuu uuuuuu uuuuuu uuuuuu will get you there . . . along with a stockpile of weapons not to be believed! If you want somewhat less sweeping help, you can actually haggle with merchants by pressing the A and B buttons at the same time when you visit a shop.

John Elway's Quarterback: This shortcut only works when you're playing the computer, but hey—it's fun to execute and watch. When it's time to pick a play, go to the normal/reverse box and do nothing. When time runs out, your quarterback and wide receivers will be fleeter than ever! It's then a simple matter to get a touchdown by snapping the ball, pressing the B button to pass, then scooting up the sidelines into the end zone.

Star Soldier: Put the cartridge in but don't turn it on. On the first controller press down the A and B buttons, and at the same time push the joystick left and up. Simultaneously push down and right with the second controller joystick. Got that? Now, with your third hand (or someone else's hand, in case you've only got two—or even with your toes), turn on the game and hit the first controller's Select button ten times. The screen will break up for a moment, after which press Start on controller one, then Select. What have all your efforts earned you? A super-laser! It may not be worth it, strategically, but you'll be a better person for having contorted yourself to punch in everything correctly. If that isn't thrilling enough, fill your holster to overflowing with this code. During the title screen mode, hit the Select button ten times on controller one. Next, simultaneously press down and right on controller two, and also press up and left on controller one. Find a free finger (or have a friend handy) and press Start on controller one.

DuckTales: Not all the walls are solid. Just thought we'd mention that, in case you hadn't figured it out. Some other beginner's tips: In the Amazon, you'll encounter a statue in the early going (after you descend the Vine). Move the platform so it's beside the statue, then hop up to access a pair of hidden rooms. (Moving it, like all key maneuvers, is accomplished by pressing the B button while pushing the controller left or right. This moves Scrooge's Cane like a golf club.) After you leave the underground area and ascend, you'll soon be harassed by the Bee. When you are, face right when Launchpad arrives. The Bee will leave you alone. Cross the collapsing bridge (with jumps, so you don't fall and die!), climb the Vine, head right, and after making your way through a narrow passageway, uncover a Treasure Chest by using the Pogo. When you do, pogo off the Chest to expose a secret tunnel above. It'll take you right to the end of the level. In Transylvania, hit the armor there twice for Cake. Note: the Ghosts from the RIPs can't be beaten. Just get out of their way!

Faxanadu: Skip the lessons in magic and judo.

They're not worth the cost. You'll figure out how to master these soon enough.

Tecmo Bowl: Give yourself the ultimate challenge by playing the computer with this code: 5B7FBFA3. What's so ultimate about this? Try it, and you'll be playing . . . yourself!

Dragon Warrior: Concentrate on the following goals in each level. One: Kill Slimes for Experience. Two: Ditto, though you should take on the tougher Red Slimes here. Three: Begin trekking north and/or west. Four: Become familiar with the east. Five: Stock up on magic in Kol.

Zelda II: The question most frequently asked by readers writing in about this game is how to get the Hammer. Okay. It's a long haul, but bear with us. Go to Saria, head to the forest in the northeast, have a heart-to-heart with the hermit Bagu (who will tell you how to cross the river), then wade to the other side. Upon reaching the lovely Death Mountain, you'll find about a quadrillion caves. Always pick the cave-mouths in the east. If there aren't any, enter the ones in the south. That'll get you through this very confusing labyrinth. When you finally reach a field with a hole (near a graveyard), enter. The Hammer will soon be yours, hero! Before you go into the caves, though, be certain to have given a Sarian the lost mirror. That's the only way you can get the Life Spell, which is crucial for getting through here. Another handy tip for *Zelda II* (and *Zelda I,* for that matter) is this. If you want to do a fast game-save, hit pause, then simultaneously press the A button and up on the control pad of the second controller. Nice, huh?

Legacy of the Wizard: Here's a spiffy code. Like the piano works of Rachmaninoff, you'll need more than two hands to input it. At the title screen, hold the A and B buttons and press right and up, all on controller two. Hold left and down, and the Select button, all on controller one. Then hit Start on controller one. You'll hear a wonderful musical note. Playing Roas, go to the first shop (the one in the tree, not far from where you started). Go to the Crystal, hit the A button, and never mind what the shopkeeper says about not having enough gold. He'll give you armor for free! But that's not all! Go back home after you leave the shop. Pick Roas and his armor again, go outside, and wait until your magic is gone. Re-enter the house, choose the character you want, and play the game. When your life meter runs dry, guess what? It'll fill up again, magically! In fact, it'll do so three times.

1943: P8XGD will take you to level eight.

Predator: There are two cave entrances at the end of the eighth level. The bottom one simply leads to level nine. The top is a warp entrance which shoots you farther ahead than that! Also, whenever you encounter the poison-spitting plants, take whatever losses you get from the toxins and run. You'll get murdered if you try to tackle the plant itself.

Commando: During the title screen, do the following on controller two: press left three times quickly, B two times, A four times, right once on the control pad, then hit Start. This will reveal all the Ladders!

Kid Niki: Neat move in stage three. Wait for

the third cloud passing vertically. Blast the bird, let the cloud continue to the top, and when it gets there, push up on the controller and leap off the cliff. You'll end up in a terrific hidden room!

Back to the Future: The only important tip we have is to stay away from the game. It's like *Paper Boy,* but without the fun. A major disappointment.

RBI Baseball: This is a fun thing to do, with no strategic value whatsoever. During the title screen, press the A and B buttons and Start, and the game's programmers will appear.

Track and Field II: If you want to jump ahead to the sixth-, seventh-, and eighth-day competitions, use the following codes, respectively: XAXF6VJNC, TAIIKUJ5I, and 4ZIIPJJ5S.

Legacy of the Wizard: Here's a code that will load you with enough weapons to destroy an army of Great Dragons: C4TB RSSH 6RXC 1TJH (that's "one") CUTK 3NFT YWMC WJVU.

As for the Ninja Turtles, some of you have been asking for a more complete rundown of the early stages to help you get started. Here's a quick overview of a good way to tackle the first level, and a healthy chunk of the second, to get you going.

To begin, use Michaelangelo and go left and down, to the right, and enter the second sewer on the right. Fight the boss at the end using Donatello, leave by the door, and go up into the building for Pizza. Still using Donatello (so you'll have the Stick), stay on the bottom floor and poke the Stick up through the floor to kill the monsters above . . . without putting yourself in any danger. Go up, leave, pass the first sewer opening and go to the one in the upper left. There's Pizza here. There are also a lot of enemies here; if you get hurt, go back to the Pizza building and stock up.

Continue on as Donatello. When you clear the building, go down and right into the building there. Stay on the upper levels of the first floor. Climb the second Ladder, then the third. Go left, staying on the upper levels. Climb the Ladder at the very end.

There are a lot of monsters in the top room; just slash your way through. Get the Pizza at the right side, on top, step across the gap near the door—don't try jumping, a simple walk across will do it—and leave.

Dive into the water and defuse the bombs, as described in the last book.

When you begin the next level, enter the Party Wagon and go into the building on the upper right for Pizza, which you'll find in the upper right. When you reach the first gap in the second floor, don't willy-nilly jump across; stop at the very edge and take a small jump. There's a full Pizza on the second floor, far right, and Anti-Foot Clan Missiles on the third floor, upper left.

When you leave the building, go down the left side, cut right, then travel down along the river and then along the park. When you hit the river at the bottom, go right, up, and across. Enter the second (that is, rightmost) building there to free a prisoner, then go to the building on its left. Get Boomerangs and Rope in here, then climb and go to the rooftop . . . keeping your eyes peeled for a full Pizza.

See our last book for a continuation from here! By way of measuring your success, you should have earned approximately 100,000 points by now.

Lastly, a boy-is-our-face-red admission. We spoke in error in our coverage of *Bionic Commando* in the first book! We said the last guy couldn't be beaten . . . and that just isn't so! What we meant to say was that the guy couldn't be beaten *easily*. Somehow, a word got lost. Thanks to Jay Buya and a zillion others who pointed out our bionic boo-boo.

We hope to see you soon in (a mistake-free!) Volume IV. There should be plenty of terrific new games out by then: *Double Dragon II: The Revenge; Gradius II;* and *Super Mario Bros. 3* among them. The story and action in *Double Dragon II: The Revenge* are basically rehashes of the first game, though the player gets some new moves. Unlike *Lifeforce,* which was a companion game rather than a true sequel to *Gradius, Gradius II* is much more like the original in layout, characters, and design. As for *Super Mario Bros. 3,* the Kuppas have turned the rulers of eight realms into animals, and Mario or Luigi must find the magic wand that can restore them . . . and also rescue the Princess. The lands through which they must travel include Grass Land, Desert Hill, Ocean Side, Big

Island, The Sky, Ice Land, The Pipe Maze, and Kuppa Castle.

They're all as good as they sound!

With luck, we'll see you again so we can share what we've learned about them!